A Comprehensive Study
of Tang Poetry I

Tang poetry is one of the most valuable cultural inheritances of Chinese history. Its distinctive aesthetics, delicate language, and diverse styles constitute great literature in itself, as well as a rich topic for literary study. This two-volume set constitutes a classic analysis of Tang poetry in the "Golden Age" of Chinese poetry (618–907 CE).

In this volume, the author provides a general understanding of poetry in the "High Tang" era from a range of perspectives. Starting with an in-depth discussion of the Romantic tradition and historical context, the author focuses on poetic language patterns, Youth Spirit, maturity symbols, and prototypes of poetry. The author demonstrates that the most valuable part of Tang poetry is how it can provide people with a new perspective on every aspect of life.

This book will appeal to researchers, scholars, and students of Chinese literature and especially of classical Chinese poetry. People interested in Chinese culture more widely will also benefit from this book.

Lin Geng was a literary historian, a scholar in ancient Chinese literature, and a modern poet. He was a professor and doctoral supervisor of Peking University. His poetic and rational qualities interact in his writing and research, forming a distinct characteristic rarely seen in the literary world.

China Perspectives

The *China Perspectives* series focuses on translating and publishing works by leading Chinese scholars, writing about both global topics and China-related themes. It covers Humanities & Social Sciences, Education, Media and Psychology, as well as many interdisciplinary themes.

This is the first time any of these books have been published in English for international readers. The series aims to put forward a Chinese perspective, give insights into cutting-edge academic thinking in China, and inspire researchers globally.

To submit proposals, please contact the Taylor & Francis Publisher for China Publishing Programme, Lian Sun (Lian.Sun@informa.com)

Titles in literature currently include:

Seven Lectures on Wang Guowei's Renjian Cihua
Florence Chia-Ying Yeh

A Companion to Shen Congwen
Sihe Chen, Gang Zhou, Jeffrey Kinkley

Keywords in Western Literary Criticism and Contemporary China
Volume 1
Hu Yamin

Keywords in Western Literary Criticism and Contemporary China
Volume 2
Hu Yamin

A Comprehensive Study of Tang Poetry I
Lin Geng

A Comprehensive Study of Tang Poetry II
Lin Geng

For more information, please visit https://www.routledge.com/China-Perspectives/book-series/CPH

A Comprehensive Study of Tang Poetry I

Lin Geng

LONDON AND NEW YORK

This book is published with financial support from the Chinese Fund for the Humanities and Social Sciences.

First edition published 2021
by Routledge
2 Park Square, Milton Park, Abingdon, Oxon, OX14 4RN

and by Routledge
52 Vanderbilt Avenue, New York, NY 10017

Routledge is an imprint of the Taylor & Francis Group, an informa business

© 2021 Lin Geng

Translated by Wang Feng (Yangtze University)

The right of Lin Geng to be identified as author of this work has been asserted by him in accordance with sections 77 and 78 of the Copyright, Designs and Patents Act 1988.

All rights reserved. No part of this book may be reprinted or reproduced or utilised in any form or by any electronic, mechanical, or other means, now known or hereafter invented, including photocopying and recording, or in any information storage or retrieval system, without permission in writing from the publishers.

Trademark notice: Product or corporate names may be trademarks or registered trademarks, and are used only for identification and explanation without intent to infringe.

English Version by permission of The Commercial Press.

British Library Cataloguing-in-Publication Data
A catalogue record for this book is available from the British Library

Library of Congress Cataloging-in-Publication Data
A catalog record has been requested for this book

ISBN: 978-0-367-64414-7 (hbk)
ISBN: 978-0-367-64480-2 (pbk)
ISBN: 978-1-003-12472-6 (ebk)

Typeset in Times New Roman
by codeMantra

Contents

Preface to the Chinese edition	vi
Foreword to the Chinese edition	viii
Translator's notes	xxviii

1	Chen Zi'ang and the Jian'an Spirit: the romantic tradition in ancient Chinese poetry	1
2	The High Tang Atmosphere	20
3	Symbols at the peak of the Tang poetry	42
4	How did landscape poetry come into being?	55
5	Language of the Tang poetry	68
6	Metrical patterns of the Tang poetry	86
7	Vitality and new prototypes of poetry	97
	Postscript to the Chinese edition	106
	Appendix: Mr Lin Geng's academic chronology	107
	Index	117

Preface to the Chinese edition

Why do I particularly love the Tang poetry?

When I was in primary school, all the texts I read were in classical Chinese. So I read and recited some classical Chinese poems—among them there was Li Shen's "Pity for Peasants": "Hoeing in the Sun at midday, / They drop their sweat on the clay. / Who knows each grain on the plate / Is out of work hard and great?" Sometimes when I or other children drop rice on the table, we were often told how we should cherish the rice and how hard peasants' farming is. I understood these facts; however, I always felt this poem was more impressive. At that time, I did not know what the Tang poetry is, but now I know its excellence. It is easy to understand and impressive. To be easy is not difficult; however, it's difficult to make it impressive. What is admirable is that I still feel renewed in reading the poems again long after I had memorised them by heart when I was small. It is not the long-known facts that are fresh, but the indescribable feeling. It seems that I am refreshing my understanding of the world in re-reading this poem. This is due to the difference between the artistic language and concepts. Such a fresh sense of understanding lies not only in the works with strong ideas, but in ordinary good poems. For example, Meng Haoran's "Spring Dawn" reads: "Spring sleep is woken at dawn hours / When birds are chirping there and here. / The night wind and rain in my ear, / Fallen are how many flowers?" What an invigorating experience of seeing the blue sky after the rain, and how pure it is when the subtle melancholy of the fallen flowers is washed away. Flowers always fall in the end, and fallen flowers are always pitiable. This is how spring comes and goes in blooming and fallen flowers. How to understand such a world? It seems like a new enlightenment. The most valuable part of the Tang poetry lies in its enlightenment of people in every aspect of life with the most novel experience. Its energetic spirit, and simple but profound language make it the perfect achievement in the history of classical Chinese poetry. Li Bai's (also Li Po, Li Tai-po, etc. 701–762) "Song of the Hengjiang River" says: "People say Hengjiang is good, / But you say Hengjiang is evil. / The river wind can blow down a hill in three days; / Its white waves are higher than the Waguan tower". In the face of such a

Preface to the Chinese edition vii

breath-taking and spectacular scenery, what do you think of the Hengjiang River? Is it good or evil? It forces you to understand the world by yourself. The Tang poetry is thus always fresh, even read 100 times. It is the fresh understanding that helps the Tang poets to have described the mountains and rivers of our home country so magnificent and gorgeous. As a part of Nature, mountains and rivers are almost the same through thousands of years; however, why are they so fascinating in the Tang poetry? That's why I particularly love the Tang poetry.

China is known as a country of poetry, and the Tang poetry is the most beautiful flower in it. Its abundant creativity and fresh understanding are artistic achievements in the splendid ancient Chinese culture we are always proud of. We do not read the Tang poetry today for imitation, because imitation will never make people feel the originality. Innumerous people imitated the Tang poetry, but their imitations have already been forgotten for long. However, the Tang poetry is still so fresh. We read the Tang poetry to make our mental state reinvigorated, powerful, and full of vitality. Such a mental state is helpful for our understanding of the world around us, which is limitless and infinite. The Tang poetry, therefore, like every beautiful classical artistic creation, has been inspiring all the people throughout history.

Originally published in *People's Daily*, 21 June 1982

Foreword to the Chinese edition

Lin Geng's Poetic Thoughts and Academic Contributions

Zhong Yuankai

Born in Minhou County, Fujian Province, Lin Geng (1910–2006), alias Jingxi, was a famous modern poet and a scholar in classical Chinese literature. After graduating from the Department of Chinese Language and Literature of Tsinghua University in 1933, he began to work at his alma mater as a teaching assistant of Mr Zhu Zhiqing. Once a professor at Xiamen University and Yenching University, and in the Department of Language and Literature at Peking University, he had major academic interests in *Chuci*,[1] the Tang poetry, and the history of Chinese literature. His works include *A Study of Poet Qu Yuan and His Works*, *A Comprehensive Study of Tang Poetry*, *A Brief History of Chinese Literature*, and *Talks on Journey to the West*.

A distinctive feature of Lin Geng's lifelong career is that his life of new poetry writing was closely accompanied by his academic career. Among modern scholars, only a few are simultaneously engaged in creative works.[2] However, Lin Geng stands out not only for his long life of creative writing, but for his idea that creation and academics are not unrelated fields. Instead, consciously starting from the creation of new poetry, he integrated the two and drew experience and nutrients from the academic study on literary history. He admitted that he "had a career in teaching but was devoted to writing" and that his research interests were "devoted to the mystery of literary and artistic creation in the field of classical literature research".[3] As early as in the 1940s, he said that "creating the future has a greater responsibility

---

1 *Chuci*, variously translated as *Chu Ci, Ch'u Tz'u, Elegies of the South, The Songs of the South, The Songs of Chu*, etc., is an anthology of ancient Chinese poetic songs traditionally attributed mainly to Qu Yuan (340–278 BCE) and Song Yu (c. 298–c. 222 BCE).
2 It is nearly 70 years from 1932 when Lin Geng started with his poem collection "Night" as his graduation thesis to 2000 when his poem collection *Reverie in Space* in his late years was published by Peking University Press.
3 Lin Geng. "Mourning Brother Zuxiang", *Historical Materials of New Literature*, 1995 (1).

Foreword to the Chinese edition ix

than studying the history", and that "all the discussions of the past are just a mission for the future, and all the understanding of arts is beneficial to writing".[4] In the 1990s, he reiterated,

> Scholars studying classical literature in past dynasties mostly focused on the past. However, I aim for the future in writing literary history to promote new literature. I experienced the New Culture Movement (mid-1910s to 1920s) after the May Fourth Movement (4 May 1919). I write new poems, and my major interest is in new poetry. In fact, the history of Chinese literature is centred on poetry. Its study provides an ideal window and examples to explore the mystery of poetic aesthetics and the development of poetic language. Thus, in studying classical literature, I always hope to find a practical and valuable way for the development of new literature, especially new poetry, and to enrich our creation today with the help of ancient cultural heritage.[5]

If creativity requires talent, then the communication between academics and creative writing needs more ambition and wisdom. However, such talent, ambition, and wisdom are beyond ordinary scholars. As a poet who grew up under the enlightenment of the May Fourth New Culture Movement, Lin Geng's faith in new poetry has always been unswerving. New poetry based on vernacular Chinese originally appeared as the opposite of classical Chinese poetry. Therefore, the communication between new poetry writing and academic studies on classical poetry is naturally endowed with a profound significance on how to make reality and tradition, innovation and inheritance, phenomena and laws achieve a dialectical integration in the process of bringing forth the new through the old. It is this process that has made Lin Geng's academic character and academic contribution outstanding and extraordinary.

Lin Geng was a tireless cultivator and explorer in the field of new poetry. He persists in theoretical thinking while writing. His perception of writing and theoretical insights are combined into his unique poetic thoughts, from which many of his academic achievements are crystallised. Therefore, starting with his poetic thoughts, we can more clearly identify his academic lines of thought and understand his academic achievements and significance.

The vitality of poetry originates from the creation of life, which is the most philosophical aspect of Lin Geng's poetic thoughts. He believed that poetry "is, therefore, a call to life, enlivening all the lifeless with the source of life, and awakening the feelings of life in all the most uninteresting places" (269);[6] "Art is not the ornament of life, but the awakening of life; artistic language

---

4 Lin Geng. *Asking for Directions*, Peking University Press, 1984, 190.
5 Lin Geng. *Metrics of New Poems and the Poeticisation of Language*, Economic Daily Publishing House, 2000, 162.
6 Cited from the Chinese edition of this book. The following page numbers from the Chinese edition will be cited in-text without additional notes.

x   *Foreword to the Chinese edition*

does not aim to be more elegant, but more primitive as if the language is newly born" (282). Of course, his words contain his understanding of creation. The joy of life that the creation of new poems brought to him is unforgettable. He has fondly recalled the "unparalleled excitement" after writing his first poem "Night", and the bitterness and sweetness in writing "Dawn". Such perceptions of creation make "the creation of life" accumulate into the core of his poetics. He wrote a motto for himself after the completion of "Night": "A little spark can start a fire that burns the entire prairie / Too much ash is useless / I will explore why a little spark burns a prairie / And trace the beginning of all beginnings", which vividly demonstrates his firm will in exploring the origin and mystery of the creation of life. This ideological core not only runs through his new poetry creation, but determines his academic interests, value orientation, and academic paths and methods. His research on classical Chinese literature focuses on creativity. He once said that "In studying literary history and classical literature, I look into its creativity with 'my heart in creation'", and that

> I am most excited in the era with the strongest creativity, believing that it is the most promising time for literature. I put creation in the first place, so when I collect materials of literary history, I also search for those that best explain creation.[7]

For example, his *A Brief History of Chinese Literature* takes creativity as an important yardstick for choosing the level of detail. Lin Geng took Qu Yuan's *Chuci*, and the Tang poetry as his research focus all his life. In an interview, he said, "Even my study of *Chuci* at the earliest was done from the angle of literary creation to explore what role *Chuci* played in the whole history of poetry development".[8] Similarly, the Tang poetry also became his research focus because of its "rich creativity". Striving for creativity, Lin Geng put the texts of works first while the writers second in his study of literary history, because "only literary works embody the writers' literary creation" and "writers are determined by their works". Creativity has become an important yardstick for choosing and evaluating different works in his academic research.

Lin Geng held that poetry mainly expresses the inner feelings rather than the external world, and the pursuit of ideals should be an essential character of poetry. Lin Geng once said that among the three elements of literary works, the first is "the fundamental human emotions that are unchanged from ancient times; therefore, when we read the masterpieces, we will feel the same emotions with the ancients".[9] He also said that "more permanent

---

7 Lin Geng and Zhang Ming. "The World is Searching for the Traces of Beauty", *Literature and Art Research*, 2003 (4).

8 Ibid.

9 Lin Geng. *Asking for Directions*, 172.

and universal sentiments are hidden behind temporary emotions" in poetry, and that the universality of arts lies in "the permanent sentiments beyond time and space" (329). Lin Geng's new poetry writing focuses on this. In the 1930s, when he was confronted with criticism that his poetry could not "grasp the reality" or "achieve an accurate social understanding", he wrote an article, replying that "I think 'content' is the most fundamental emotion of life; it is an affection for freedom, love, beauty, loyalty, bravery, and innocence, or sadness without them; the sadness, even desperate, shows that it is uncompromising, and forever facing the precious soul!"[10] Obviously, "the fundamental emotion of life", the expression of the spiritual world, is the core of poetry, and the transcendence of ideal over reality is essential and inherent in poetry. He said that "the purpose of art is to bring people to a higher ideal, rather than to make them dependent on life" (359), that "literature and art, therefore, do not await but create the time. Thus, poetry is a lofty feeling of the time", and that "the vitality of poetry... must be achieved from the lowest to the loftiest" (268, 269). Emotions are related to the category of "loftiness", which shows that Lin Geng attaches more importance to transcending the ordinary emotional texture and emotional intensity. Some critics also found from this point of view the value of his poems at that time in that "The Youth Spirit prevalent in the May Fourth Movement generally declined in the 1930s; however, in Lin Geng's poems, it showed a new vigour and advancement".[11]

Lin Geng concentrated his ideal of poetic beauty into a phrase, that is, "a fresh sense of understanding",[12] which mainly refers to the perfect combination of "its energetic spirit" and the "simple but profound language" in poetry (1). The function of poetry is to make us "always have new emotions in our lives, and always be affected by the tide of emotions" and to bring back the "joy and reasons of life" that have long been lost (266); thus, the real charm of poetry is "the soberness of emotions, the vitality of senses, and the sensitivity to all new things" (287). Lin Geng often uses "the Youth Spirit" to refer to the grandeur of poetry. If its connotation is "vigorous, creative, upward, youthful, even sad and painful, it still belongs to the youth", then it is, in fact, an aesthetic concept similar to "the fresh sense of understanding". However, "the Youth Spirit" as a poetic metaphor more highlights its spiritual characteristics.

When new poetry was in its infancy during the May Fourth Movement, modern romantic literary thoughts greatly helped the poetry circle to innovate at that time, and these thoughts became the conceptual backbone and foundation of Lin Geng's poetics. For example, his understanding of the

---

10 Lin Geng. "Spring Wilderness and Windows: Self-Postscript", quoted in Peng Qingsheng and Fang Ming. "The Annalistic Record of Lin Geng's Works", *Journal of Huaiyin Normal University*, 2003 (4).

11 Sun Yushi. "On the Spiritual World of Lin Geng's Poems in the 1930s", in *A Collection of Nourishing Rains*, People's Literature Publishing House, 2005, 286.

12 Lin Geng and Zhang Ming. "The World Is Searching for the Traces of Beauty".

xii *Foreword to the Chinese edition*

nature, expressions, and functions of poetry, his view of creativity as the touchstone of art, and his idea of naturalness as an important criterion for weighing the value of poetry are closely related to the trend of romanticism. Lin Geng claimed that "I belong to the romantic school, which is probably the best and most normal school in the history of poetry".[13] However, the essence of romanticism lies in its special promotion of subjects' spirit, that is, emphasising the spiritual temperament and spiritual characteristics of poetry, and all those contained in poetry such as the full, youthful disposition, the extraordinary ideal, and the heroic characters that inspire and strengthen the will of life, which are considered the fundamentals for the fresh understanding of poetry. Lin Geng wrote in his own preface to *A History of Chinese Literature* published in Xiamen University Press that

> I think the characteristics of the time should be the forms of thoughts and the emotions of life. The High Tang (713–766) and the Northern Song Dynasty (960–1127) are both peaceful and prosperous times with little difference in life. However, the Tang people's sentiment of emancipation, lofty pursuit and longing in the journey of life were not seen in the Song Dynasty (960–1279); this caused the division in literature and arts between the Tang and Song Dynasties.[14]

Lin Geng's poetic thoughts have made his study of the Tang poetry a comprehensive interpretation of the poetic peak from the romantic poetic viewpoint. His modern interpretation of the High Tang poetry is based on his grasp of its most distinct spiritual temperament and his overall comprehension of the aesthetic grandeur it has reached. In elaborating the inheritance and development of the High Tang Atmosphere on the basis of the Jian'an Spirit and the essential characteristics of the High Tang poetry, he has grasped its inner spirit mainly from his aesthetic perceptions. For example, he believes that the spiritual essence of the Jian'an Spirit is a "free-running romantic temperament with bright images full of prospect", and the "power of emancipation" it reflects thus constitutes the backbone of the High Tang Atmosphere, which "is a more abundant development of the Jian'an Spirit" (34–36). If the keynote of Jian'an literature is "characterised by the desolate and high-pitched singing" of "'the bleak autumn wind' and 'the sad wind on the high terrace'" because of its time (238), the High Tang shows "a kind of self-confident and delightful prospect (35)". Thus, the High Tang Atmosphere refers to

> the burgeoning atmosphere in poetry, which is not only due to its grand development, but more importantly, the characteristic burgeoning ideas and feelings which cannot be separated from that era. The High Tang Atmosphere is, therefore, a reflection of the spirit of the High Tang.

(28)

13 Lin Geng. *Metrics of New Poems and the Poeticisation of Language*, 159.
14 Lin Geng. *A Brief History of Chinese Literature*, Peking University Press, 1995, 726.

Foreword to the Chinese edition xiii

Chen Zi'ang, as a bridge between the Jian'an Spirit and the High Tang Atmosphere, became "the pioneer of the High Tang poetry circle" and began its prelude because his poems enhanced the "heroic temperament for breaking through the status quo" with "a passion for ideals" (31–32).

This spirit was peculiar to the High Tang. "This kind of melody is rare before. However, in the Tang poetry, it has become the major theme with heart-moving affection", while "the melody of spring since the Mid-Tang (766–835) and Late Tang (618–907) has been shrouded in a weak tenderness and dreamlike pursuit" (240). In the Song Dynasty, "a kind of middle-aged men's need of personal integrity and a mood close to the pure autumn atmosphere have become the common keynotes of poetry, prose, drawings, and even philosophy such as Neo-Confucianism" (362).

Lin Geng's understanding of the spiritual essence of the High Tang Atmosphere is based not only on a diachronic historical examination by tracing back to the Jian'an Spirit until Chen Zi'ang's tradition, but on a synchronic comparison of different typical poets in the High Tang, specifically represented by Li Bai, Wang Wei (also Wang Mojie, 699 / 701–761), and Du Fu (also Tu Fu, 71–770). They have their typical characteristics at the peak of poetry: Li Bai is "a typical model at the height of the poetic era", Wang Wei is "a more comprehensive model" (117), and Du Fu is "an epitome and the last great poet in the High Tang poetry" (151). "If Li Bai is a typical model in pursuit of what will be available, then Wang Wei is a general reflection of what is available" (124). Different in styles and achievements, the three representative poets also expressed the common youth melody of the High Tang.

In *The Poet Li Bai* published in 1954, Lin Geng highlighted the spirit of the High Tang represented by the poet. Because of his "sense as a commoner" and independence, Li Bai intensively expressed "the lively singing of the common people emancipated from the aristocratic literature, and the free and unique singing emancipated from the feudal ethics" (212). Li Bai's "optimistic and high-spirited quality, enlightening prospects, unquenchable thirst for liberation, rich and distinct imagination, plain and heavenly expressions, and profound thoughts in simple language" (229) became the strongest voice of that era. In the early 1950s, the study of Li Bai was once in a state of "aphasia", but Lin Geng was not restrained by the trend at that time. He vigorously praised Li Bai's romantic spirit and called it the "emblematic singing" of the High Tang (229). He cultivated a new field and played a leading role in the study of Li Bai. After its publication, it was reprinted nine times in only a few years. In 2000, Shanghai Chinese Classics Publishing House wrote in the "Note for the New Edition" that "the basic issues about Li Bai's works since the reform and opening up of China have all been derived from this short but fruitful and lasting book", demonstrating its considerable academic weight.

Lin Geng's interpretation of Wang Wei and Du Fu embodied his unique insight and understanding. Wang Wei has long been regarded as a landscape poet represented by the *Rim River Collection* in his later years; however, Lin xiv *Foreword to the Chinese edition*

Geng thought that "these lonely works in his later years were just a part of his poetic life, not representing all his achievements at that time" (130). Wang Wei wrote many frontier fortress poems, such as "Song of Longxi", "Song of Youth", and "Song of Longtou", in which "such romantic and heroic feeling of these young roaming swordsmen running to the frontier fortress is the embodiment of the Youth Spirit of the High Tang" (120–121). Even his landscape poems are not constrained in a quiet corner, but have a broad space, lively vitality, and fresh spirit. Lin Geng pointed out that in general works on literary history, "to classify the High Tang poets into landscape poets and frontier fortress poets would have hindered us from understanding a poet in an all-round way" (120). The reason why Wang Wei is a "comprehensive model" in the High Tang is that in his poems, "everywhere is the lively spring, and everywhere is the fresh green, which is seen in the air and drizzle, constituting the overall atmosphere of Wang Wei's poetry" (126). Since the Song and Yuan (1280–1368) Dynasties because of historical reasons, people "have long lost a comprehensive understanding of Wang Wei's poetry" (130). However, Lin Geng restored the poet's original features closely linked with the time. Du Fu's poems after the An Shi Rebellion (755–763) have been well known for reflecting the suffering of the time. Lin Geng, however, sensed the persistent pursuit and hope of spring in the chaotic period from his poems such as "Happy at the Spring Night Rain", "Washing Weapons and Horses", and "On the Army's Recapturing of Henan and Hebei". This is a release and echo of the "Youth Spirit" in a special form. For example, "Washing Weapons and Horses" is "literally a long symphonic poem with the melody of spring, bursting out the feelings that were suppressed deep inside", and smoothly forms "a triumphant and everlasting masterpiece of rejuvenation" (239). Also, "On the Army's Recapturing of Henan and Hebei" sings "an unconstrained song", and "the last flowing water couplet (or complementary couplet) fully demonstrated the poet's happy mood, and the return of the melody of spring to the poet's heart". Lin Geng thus believes that "These rekindled memories of rejuvenation were temporarily suppressed in the An Shi Rebellion but never extinguished" (239–240). Even on the sad autumn songs such as "On Autumn", "Feelings on Ancient Monuments", and "Mount Climbing", Lin Geng's interpretation is that it is "precisely because the hope of rejuvenation had been so strong in his heart that once he saw clearly that it would finally be gone, he would definitely write down such mournful feelings" (240). The three representative poets reflected the universal spiritual outlook of the High Tang through their artistic individuality.

The theory of "the spirit of the time" originated from romantic philosophy. Because the High Tang is a peak era through historical integration rather than a differentiated period of many divergent paths, it is an appropriate theory to illustrate the overall style of the High Tang literature and art, especially of poetry. Through the diachronic analysis and synchronic comparison, Lin Geng made the "High Tang Atmosphere" a vivid and three-dimensional generalisation of the spirit of the time.

Foreword to the Chinese edition xv

This interpretation firmly rooted in the poetic understanding of the texts is full of flesh and blood rather than pale and empty. Lin Geng, as a poet, demonstrated his superior ability beyond that of ordinary people. His poetic creation made him deeply realise the characteristics of poetic language, that is, "to understand all the potential forces in language images, and to combine these potential forces with the meaning in concepts", and "full of affection and inspiration, it is not constrained by words" (301–302). Therefore, the key to poetry interpretation lies in grasping "the abundant potential capacity" of the poetic language (284). For example, in his quotation of Li Bai's "Song of the Hengjiang River": "People say Hengjiang is good, / But you say Hengjiang is evil. / The river wind can blow down a hill in three days; / Its white waves are higher than the Waguan tower". His commentaries are: "Facing the dangerous surging waves, he wrote out such a spectacular scene, making it a grand song of the era, similar to the soul-stirring 'Hard are the Trails of Shu,'" and "the overwhelming brilliant image shows the growth of an era's character that can withstand the surging waves" (50). Li Bai's "Bringing in the Wine" ends with "And kill with you thousands of years of sorrow". Lin Geng said, "If we think that 'white hair of ten thousand metres,' and 'kill with you thousands of years of sorrow' are only about the huge amount and endurance of sorrow, we are still at the literal level. A deeper understanding of the image should focus on its fullness and vigour, which is the real accomplishment of the High Tang Atmosphere" (51). He also quoted Wang Changling's "Seeing off Xin Jian at the Lotus Tower": "When cold rain came to River Wu at night, / I bid farewell at Mount Chu alone at dawn. / If my friends in Luoyang ask about me: / A piece of ice heart is in a jade pot". His commentary is:

> The High Tang Atmosphere is full and burgeoning because it is abundant in every corner of life; it seems not exaggerating when it uses exaggeration in 'white hair of ten thousand metres', and it seems not small in 'a piece of ice heart in a jade pot.' Just like a small dandelion, it represents the whole spring world. It is exquisite and thorough, but still dense. It is sorrowful in a thousand ways but still open-hearted. Rooted in the great enthusiasm of life and the sensitivity of new things,… it brings sunny, rich, and healthy aesthetic attainments.
>
> (52)

Meng Haoran's "Spring Dawn" seems to rest on a sad sentiment according to its order of words, but Lin Geng's interpretation is "What an invigorating experience of seeing the blue sky after the rain, and how pure it is when the subtle melancholy of the fallen flowers is washed away" (1). The specific emotions expressed in these poems might differ in thousands of ways, but Lin Geng is able to sharply grasp the keynote. His poetic perception has the distinct characteristics of being "not determined by reasoning, or constrained by words" (Yan Yu's *Azure Stream Poetic Remarks*), that is, xvi *Foreword to the Chinese edition*

not weighing and balancing on the literal interpretation, nor sticking to the logical order as in the prose, but directly exploring the most intrinsic characteristics of the "literary mind" and "poetic sentiment" of poetry, that is, focusing on the fullness of emotions, the vividness of images, and the rhythm of melodies at a deeper level, in which the spiritual outlook of the time can be traced and identified. In "Essays on Poems" in the Chinese edition of this book, some appreciation essays are compiled with academic articles. This special editing style shows that the author attaches great importance to the textual interpretation because the only way to understand the spiritual features of poetry is to have an accurate and thorough understanding of the integrity of the sensibility and rationality of the poetic text. However, if completely divorced from sensible interpretation, it is easy to produce a misreading that loses the essence while focusing on the marginal aspects. When Lin Geng interpreted and studied poetry with a "poetic attitude", the grandeur he attained naturally transcended scholars who are accustomed to interpreting and explaining poetry with a "non-poetic attitude". The integration of academic character and aesthetic disposition, the unity of poetic perception and rational analysis, and the mastery of poetry and history have become the distinct academic personality and characteristics of his "academic scholarship as a poet".

To summarise the overall outlook of a poem, Lin Geng proposed "atmosphere", an aesthetic tradition of poetry in ancient China since the Tang and Song Dynasties. Jiaoran and Yin Fan in the Tang Dynasty, and Jiang Kui and Yan Yu in the Song Dynasty all used it to interpret the High Tang poetry. Yan Yu also used "atmosphere" to metaphorise the continuous historical connection between the High Tang and Jian'an, and considered the "Jian'an Spirit" and the "High Tang Atmosphere" as ideal models of poetic beauty. Lin Geng also made a modern interpretation of traditional literary theories when he expounded the "High Tang Atmosphere". For example, Yan Yu's evaluation of the Tang poetry in terms of "interest" and "ingenious enlightenment" is indescribably remarkable, while Lin Geng has demystified Yan Yu's Zen discourse and returned to its simplicity and conciseness with his perception of poetry creation and modern literature and art studies.

> However, in *Azure Stream Poetic Remarks*, the term "enlightenment" is the capture of images, the "disposition" or "interest" is the triumph of imagination, the 'thoroughness' means to directly seek profundity out of simplicity, and the "atmosphere" is about the style and manner. The word 'dense' is used to show the vitality and fullness of the style and manner, which is the reflection of the High Tang Spirit.

(47)

Yan Yu said that "The Han and Wei poems are not relying on enlightenment" while "the High Tang poets have thorough enlightenment". Lin Geng explained that

Foreword to the Chinese edition xvii

Since the Han and Wei poets did not strive to capture images, the images were simple but complete; thus, "excellent lines are difficult to find"; it's like an unexplored mine or "a chaotic atmosphere". The High Tang poets, on the other hand, endeavoured to capture and obtain the most direct and distinct images. It seems as if the mine of real gold and jade has been explored and is shining with beautiful and extraordinary brilliance, which cannot be chaotic, but is in a dense atmosphere.

(46–47)

The poet's perceptions on writing have provided him with the ability to theoretically control complexity with simplicity and cut off the flow of thoughts to be enlightened suddenly, enabling him to become familiar with the process of changing ancient speeches to thrive in a modern context. This kind of theoretical discourse transformation and the poetic interpretation of poetic texts complement each other and make the poetic aesthetic paradigm of the "High Tang Atmosphere" coruscate with new vigour and vitality.

As mentioned before, the high point and basic spirit of the May Fourth romanticism have become the major background of Lin Geng's poetics, from which he reinterpreted and expounded classical Chinese poetry. He realised the modern transformation of the aesthetic tradition of ancient Chinese poetry from this special perspective. Coincidentally, Wen Yiduo and Lin Geng are modern poets of romantic temperament, Wen's *Miscellanies of the Tang Poetry* and Lin's *A Comprehensive Study of Tang Poetry* have become far-reaching landmarks with great influence in this field because of their achievements in such a modern transformation. As a thought of writing, romanticism has gone through a gradual decay process from the peak after descending, fading, and exile from modern Chinese literary circles. However, Lin Geng, who received its direct inheritance in poetics, persisted in it and relentlessly explored with creativeness, and was shining brilliantly in academia. Such a contrast is thought-provoking.

The exploration of the mystery of poetic language constitutes another important part of Lin Geng's poetic thoughts. Most of his theoretical articles on new poetry are centred on the construction of poetic language. The focus of this poetic thought also brought ground-breaking discoveries and achievements to his academic research.

Poetic language is the focus of the new poetry circle:

Today, looking back at the new poetry circle, we find that many problems arisen are mainly centred around the language. For example, language issues include the controversy between classical Chinese poetry and vernacular poetry in the early period, the argument between free verse and metrical poetry in the late period, and the disputation in the 1950s between the form of "foot" in western languages and the form of "x-character" in Chinese.[15]

---

15 Lin Geng. *Metrics of New Poems and the Poeticisation of Language*, 16–17.

xviii *Foreword to the Chinese edition*

Having liberated itself from old style poetry, has new poetry been accomplished? In other words, "does the emancipation of poetic language only suggest prosification?"[16] Although free verse has brought about brand-new emancipation to him, Lin Geng's writing practice and theoretical thinking made him meditate profoundly. He once cited his poem "Nature" as an example. Full of mysterious cosmic consciousness, abstract and metaphysical metaphors, and free sentence patterns, it is perhaps the most modernistic free verse. However, after its writing, the poet himself could not help feeling "narrow and deep", which is in contradiction with "emancipation". Summing up the status quo of the poetry circle at that time, he said that free verse "broke away from the constraints of old poetry while grasping some new progress, in which, however, everything is sharp, deep but radical;... And the sharp, deep, and radical ways, if continue, must fall into the trend of being 'narrow'".[17] Based on this sober reflection, Lin Geng put forward the proposition that the poetic language should be emancipated twice: "since the language of new poetry has been emancipated in the waves of prose, does it still need re-emancipation?" "Re-emancipation" means "to get rid of the inherent logical habits of prose" and "to further find a more perfect form".[18] As for the process of emancipation of poetry from prose, Lin Geng called it "poeticisation".

The two-time emancipation of poetic language is a realistic subject put forward in Ling Geng's writing practice of new poetry. However, his research on the poeticisation of language has opened up a brand-new academic field. On the one hand, he devoted himself to grasping the new rhythms in the language of life, and attempted to write new metrical poems; on the other hand, he traced back the historical experience and laws in the development of the forms of Chinese poetry, and embarked on the ways of exploring the poeticisation of traditional poetic language. It can be seen that it is Lin Geng's attention to the evolution trend of new poetry that activated and promoted his unique "problem consciousness" and perspective in his academic research.

This traditional exploration is based on the belief that the creation of poetic language cannot leave the national cultural soil. Lin Geng said: "Accumulated in history, the cultural soil is a crystallization of chances and inevitability, sensibility and rationality in thousands of years", and "language is something with roots in culture".[19] "Of course, the soil should not be limited to language, but poetry is the purest art of language; the soil of language is thus particularly important".[20] In the new poetry circle with the prevailing trend of "Europeanisation", such an understanding is undoubtedly more historical.

---

16 Lin Geng. *Asking for Directions*, 1.
17 Ibid., 175.
18 Ibid., 2.
19 Lin Geng. *Metrics of New Poems and the Poeticisation of Language*, 175–176.
20 Ibid., 2.

Lin Geng discovered: "From *Chuci* to the Tang poetry, the national forms of Chinese poetry did have a similar development. It also obtained certain freedom first in the waves of prose emancipation, and then found the perfect five- or seven-character forms and had more freedom".[21] His research on the process of poeticisation also focuses on this historical period. The key points and highlights of his research on literary history rest upon how the poetic language based on the language of life constantly evolved, innovated, grew up, and matured in a tortuous course, the linguistic achievements and signs at the peak of the poetic country, and the artistic experience that can be learned from today.

In his research, Lin Geng related the "process" of poeticisation closely to the "connotation" of poeticisation. In other words, the development of the process is mainly to understand the essence of poeticisation, so as to learn from the enlightenment and reference of the tradition for today. To outline the necessary ways of transition from the old to the new in the poetry circle, he mainly discussed the maturity symbols of poeticisation from the following three aspects.

The first maturity symbol of poeticisation is the formation of the universal forms in the poetry circle. As a historical reference to new poetry, *Chuci* became the starting point of his study. *Chuci* written at the peak of prose in the pre-Qin Dynasty (2100–221 BCE) was greatly influenced by prosification. Compared with the four-character style of *Shijing*,[22] *Chuci* obviously had great emancipation. However, why did this freed poetic form become an unprecedented and incomparable phenomenon in literary history? Why is it not the form of *Chuci*, but the subsequent five- and seven-character forms that have become the universal forms of poetry? This issue has hardly been touched upon in the past studies of *Chuci* and literary history. After a comparison and contrast between *Chuci* and four-, five-, and seven-character poetry, Lin Geng pointed out that *Chuci*, a prosified product of the poetic language, brings a brand new rhythm to the poetry circle, that is, the three-character rhythm in a large number of poetic lines. Compared with the two-character rhythm of the four-character poetry in *Shijing*, this is a new leap. Different from the expression function in *Shijing*, the Chinese character "兮[xī] (a carrier sound)" in almost every line in *Chuci* functions as a pause and musical note, dividing each line into two symmetrical parts. The following five- and seven-character poetic lines inherited the characteristics of "half-pause" and three-character rhythm in *Chuci*. Nevertheless, the forms of poems in *Chuci* are not the same. There is not only the improved

---

21 Lin Geng. *Asking for Directions*, 3.
22 *Shijing*, also known as *Shih-ching*, translated variously as the *Classics of Poetry*, the *Book of Songs*, the *Book of Odes*, or simply as the *Odes* or *Poetry*. It is the oldest existing collection of classical Chinese poetry, comprising 305 works dating from the 11th to seventh centuries BCE. It is one of the "Five Classics" traditionally said to have been compiled by Kongzi (also Kong Fuzi, usually as Confucius in English, 551–479 BCE).

xx *Foreword to the Chinese edition*

form of *Shijing* in the "Ode to the Orange", but the regular form closer to the later seven-character poetry in "Nine Songs", showing that *Chuci* is a kind of transition and bridge with a new rhythm that is far from being finalised. Because it did not finish the task of "construction", the forms in *Chuci* did not become the universal forms in classical poetry. Although it can be said to be a "strange pioneer" of five- and seven-character poetry, *Chuci*, a peak of singing, is lack of follow-ups.

In the following Han Dynasty, there were both five- and seven-character poems with the basic rhythm of "the three-character end", indicating that they were from the same origin, i.e., the same new rhythm of *Chuci*. This is why five-character poetry and four-character poetry are in different eras though they differ only by one character, while five-character poetry and seven-character poetry are in the same era though they differ by two characters. Five-character poetry is a combination of the three-character pattern of *Chuci* and the two-character pattern of *Shijing*. On the original tradition and length of *Shijing*, it was more easily accepted at an early stage than seven-character poetry. Thus, it became dominant in the poetry circle at first, but it did not make the poeticisation reach its peak. It was not until the emergence of a large number of lively and fluent seven-character poems that brought full-scale prosperity to the poetry circle, because seven-character poems with an essentially simpler and more thorough three-character rhythm are more vernacular and easier to follow than five-character poems.[23]

The period from *Shijing* to *Chuci* until the Tang Dynasty when five- and seven-character poetry became fully mature spanned nearly a thousand years. This long period of historical observation provided convenience for summarising the development laws of the Chinese poetic language. Obviously, Lin Geng's academic research is synchronous with his thoughts on new poetry. For example, the proposition of the "half-pause law" began with the study of punctuation in "Crossing the River" of *Chuci*. Wen Yiduo thought that the original bamboo slips were in disorder, and could not punctuate properly, while Lin Geng thought that the half-pause law can be applied to solve the problem, and then further extended to the punctuation function of "兮" in *Chuci*. However, it is only after "the confirmation in new poetry" that it rises to be "a general characteristic of Chinese poetry".[24] In the same year of 1948, he published two articles, "The Nature of the Character '兮' in *Chuci*" and "The Forms of New Poetry Revisited". The former put forward a new interpretation of the rhythmic function of the character "兮" in *Chuci*, while the latter proposed the "half-pause law" of poetry for the first time, positing that "if a poetic line has a 'pause' in the middle, it can have rhythm". "When poetry can establish new patterns of language, it can have a new universal language, and poetic lines can have

---

23 Lin Geng. *Metrics of New Poems and the Poeticisation of Language*, 75, 99–109, 128–137.
24 Ibid., 157.

Foreword to the Chinese edition xxi

endless but steadfast forms".[25] Both of them confirm each other and develop each other, which not only strengthens Lin Geng's understanding that the language development of new poetry should focus on the issue of "construction of poetic lines", but helps him discover in an academic way the evolution rules of the forms of classical Chinese poetry centred around the form of "x-character". Scholars have studied different styles of poetry in various ways, but Lin Geng is exceptional in that he not only focused on the fixed forms, but directly explored the mystery of the growth and development of different types of poetry, from which he summed up the basic composition law of Chinese poetry, the "rhythmic pattern". Such an academic achievement is inextricably linked to his academic approach embracing the topics of the time.

The second maturity symbol of poeticisation is the visualisation of language or the abundance of images. If "the maturity of poetic forms is only a most superficial symbol of the poeticisation of language" (95), then the poeticisation of vocabulary and grammar is also worthy of great concern. The poeticisation of grammar such as the simplification or omission of function words and the formation of special syntax is conducive to the refinement and flexibility of poetic language and the foregrounding of images. The poeticisation of vocabulary is "the most intrinsic link in these steps, and it seems to be a poetic catalyst that makes a breakthrough at one point but develops into a comprehensive one" (295). From the perspective of poetic "images" to explain the poeticisation of vocabulary, Lin Geng brought brilliance to the theory about "the visualisation of language".

The perspective of "images" is also related to Lin Geng poetics. It was the 1930s when he entered the poetry circle and reached his creative peak. The modern poetic trend in that period in China, which drew on the artistic concepts and creative experience of Western Symbolism, Imagism, and Modernism, had a significant influence on his poetic creation and poetic ideas. At that time, one of the leading journals *Modern* published the translation and introduction of English and American imagist poetry, and illustrated the poetics of Imagism. This poetic trend emphasised "modern emotions in modern life" and replaced the "feelings" expressed in confession with the inner "emotions" condensed after sublimation, and substituted the spontaneous flow of passion with the combination of images and emotions. Several poetry anthologies that Lin Geng published in the 1930s were included in modern poetry by literary historians.[26] In his published article "Rhythm of Poetry", Lin Geng said: "A literary work has three basic elements: basic human emotions, the content, and feelings, which are about how an emotion falls on something, or how something produces an emo-

---

25 Lin Geng. *Asking for Directions*, 208–210.
26 Sun Yushi. *On the History of Chinese Modernist Poetry*, Peking University Press, 1999, 123–155.

xxii *Foreword to the Chinese edition*

tion". He also said that "a great element (of poetry) is about emotions, but the development of feelings is what a gardener does in the field of human spirits". Here, the "emotions" and "feelings" refer to the "new sentiment and feelings" pursued and captured by "free verses such as Symbolist poetry".[27] In the 1940s, he published "Vitality and New Prototypes of Poetry", in which he emphasised "the new feelings on new things", and reflected on the tradition of classical Chinese poetry through image symbolism, from which he expounded the importance of "new prototypes". Deep impressions of modernist poetry are obviously seen here.

With a deep understanding of the images in classical poetry and the sensitivity as a poet, Lin Geng is greatly at home flying in the world of images of ancient poetry. In fact, the "new prototypes" mentioned above are "new images". Images have to rely on new feelings to enter the poetry circle and become "poetic yearnings". Their maturity has a historical accumulation process, which is an important aspect of "language poeticisation". For example, the "zither" accompanied five-character poems and the "flute" became the bosom friend of seven-character poems, while the "wind" became the pride of the poetry circle in Jian'an and the "rain" became more and more emotional in the Tang poetry. In ci poems, such images as "pavilion", "bridge", "swing", and "railing" became prominent images for some time. These were originally used as proof of how new poems acquired new prototypes; however, they opened up a new garden.

Lin Geng has combed many times the historical tradition of the evolution of images in classical poetry. For example, Qu Yuan made the mythical "Nine Songs" more poetic rather than storytelling. After Qu Yuan's creation, "autumn wind", "the Dongting Lake", and "wooden leaves" have become the most sentimental words in the poetry circle. The "willow" has already appeared in "Minor Court Hymns: Picking Vetches", and developed deep national feelings in "Of yore I went away, / Willows would not say bye", "Verdant grass grows along the river banks; / Green willows in the garden are flourishing", and "Lush orchids grow under the window; / Plenteous willows are before the hall". Then, it had a layer of complex sentiment in the folk song "Song of Plucking Willows" in the Northern Dynasties (386–581). In the Tang poems, the willow was not only interwoven with the complex mood of "youth is happiness; parting is bitterness", but related to the nostalgia of the homeland in the frontier fortress and the yearning for spring (249–251). The images such as the "pass", "mountain", and "moon" accumulated considerable life history from the Qin and Han Dynasties to the Tang Dynasty. The depth and breadth of life feelings they aroused inspired Wang Changling's famous line "In the passes of Han under the moon from Qin", which predominated over all the frontier feelings in a thousand years.

---

27 Lin Geng. *Asking for Directions*, 167–168.

Foreword to the Chinese edition xxiii

The creation of images contributes to the emergence of perceptual factors in poetic language, which is fully demonstrated in the article "On 'Wooden Leaves'". Beginning with an investigation into the historical development of a specific language image, this article makes an accurate and detailed analysis of the rich connotation of the poetic language that is based on concepts and transcends concepts, or its perceptual characteristics. The term "wooden leaves", taking the place of "tree leaves", becomes the poets' favourite without making any difference in concept. However, in the field of artistic images, one word is worth a thousand pieces of gold. "Wooden leaves" and "tree leaves" are different in that the former are sparse and scattered, while the latter are usually luxuriant and lush; the former have a yellowish and dry feeling of falling leaves, while the latter are moist and not drifting. However, Du Fu and Huang Tingjian further created a term "falling wood", which "cleaned up the denseness suggested by the word 'leaves'". Thus, the term "wooden leaves" in "Nine Songs" is quite profound, because "it is the unity of 'wood' and 'leaves,' the interweaving of sparseness and denseness, and a distant, an affectionate, and a beautiful image", while "falling wood" is so spacious that it will "cut off the tenderness". Thus, the creation of language visualisation by such poets as Qu Yuan, Du Fu, and Huang Tingjian (also Huang Shangu) is understood and received a detailed and discerning elaboration.

Lin Geng related the poeticisation of the seemingly micro language images to the evolution of the macro history, and re-evaluated the writer's historical values from the perspective of the creation and influence of poeticisation. Why can Song Yu's "Nine Arguments" be unique among the numerous imitations of Qu Yuan? Lin Geng holds that "Nine Arguments" inherited and developed Qu Yuan's steps of poeticisation. From the breakthrough of "autumn wind", "Nine Arguments" further combined "Impoverished men lost their official positions and felt unfair" with "How sorrowful the autumn atmosphere is". Thus, it gained adherents in the poetry circle, pioneered the "Song of the Autumn Wind" by Emperor Wudi of the Han Dynasty (202 BCE–220), inspired Cao Pi's "Song of the Yan", and enlightened the Jian'an era (196–220) and even later. Therefore, Song Yu is different from those ordinary imitators and should have his status in literary history (288–296).

Lin Geng also extended the research method of "image analysis" to the discussion of the significance of landscape poetry and frontier fortress poetry. He pointed out that landscape poetry flourished for the great progress of image capturing in poetry. It is not only inspiring but combined with the poet's political aspiration, official life away from home, wandering, travelling, and home thoughts. Thus, it goes beyond ordinary subject matters and becomes "more closely related to a general national form" (81). As a new symbol of the image language, the emergence of landscape poetry has also promoted the further visualisation of allusions in poetry. "Since the development of landscape poetry, the images in allusions began not to rely entirely on the original story, but on all the objects in Nature directly taken

xxiv *Foreword to the Chinese edition*

from the living environment" (92). The significance of frontier fortress poetry lies not in a specific battlefield or battle, or in a specific time and place, but in a wide range of time and space to sing about the frontier fortress as an entirety. It is actually "an expansion of the traditional theme of wanderers, political vision, as well as landscape and scenery" (66). It is a new image of poetry that emerged in expressing the passion of the time.

"The theory of imagery" has aroused heated discussion and concern in the academic circle and the poetry circle in the 1980s. However, 20 or 30 years earlier, Lin Geng had used this method to systematically analyse the language images of classical poetry. This unprecedented study had given a freshly enlightening and pioneering theoretical explanation to an important part of language poeticisation.

The third maturity symbol of poeticisation is the realisation of the language accomplishment or aesthetic model of "profundity out of simplicity". Lin Geng summed up the language styles and achievements of the Tang poetry with "profundity out of simplicity", which is not a simple comment and description of his impression, but reflects his own aesthetic ideal, which was born and sublimated from his observation and summary of the differentiation and disputes in the new poetry circle. Shortly after the birth of the new poetry, there were two different tendencies of "profundity" and "simplicity". The vernacular poems represented by Hu Shi's *Trial Collection*, with the aim of "being plain and clear" and "writing poems like writing essays", belonged to the school of simplicity, while the early symbolic poems represented by Li Jinfa belonged to the school of profundity for their obscurity and mystery. In the 1930s, with the rise of modernist poetry, there were once again debates about "clarity" and "obscurity", and "intelligibility and unintelligibility" regarding poetic expressions. Lin Geng summed up the New Poetry Movement by dividing its development into three stages: the first is the period of getting rid of the old poetry; the second is the period of "writings centred on the journal Modern and numerous poets' free verses" when the modernist poetry was in full swing in the 1930s. This is a period of shedding the imitations from Western poetry, in which "the authors delve into profound knowledge and explore hidden things to have their own creation"; thus, "it's a period of profundity". The third stage should be a period of "going back to simplicity from profundity" and "casting off unintelligibility". Lin Geng believed that "profundity out of simplicity is a natural order and a supreme ideal".[28] His attempt to shift from the "narrow and deep" new free verses to new metrical poetry was probably driven by this ideal.

This aesthetic ideal enriched and deepened Lin Geng's understanding of the Tang poetry, especially the linguistic model of the High Tang poetry. To reach the grandeur of "profundity out of simplicity" needs many conditions. In terms of language, it's necessary to find the universal forms of poetry at

---

28 Lin Geng. *Asking for Directions*, 202–203.

Foreword to the Chinese edition xxv

first, because "the universality of forms is the emancipation of forms so that expressions can have profundity out of simplicity".[29] "When poetry can establish new patterns of language, it can have a new universal language, and poetic lines can have endless but steadfast forms. Then, in terms of form, profundity and simplicity can have new emancipation and unification".[30] Profundity out of simplicity is certainly inseparable from the visualisation of language. "Profundity" includes what is "deeply rooted in the field of images" (99). Nevertheless, the realisation of the grandeur of "profundity out of simplicity" depends, on the one hand, on the accumulation and inheritance in history, and, on the other hand, on the great creation of contemporary poets, so that poeticisation can blossom brilliantly on the traditional branches and produce fruitful results.

Lin Geng's study of the poeticisation grandeur of "profundity out of simplicity" is characterised by his discovery and exposition of the Tang people's creativeness. Lin Geng believed that classical Chinese poetry had all the forms in the Tang Dynasty, and the Tang people's creativeness was best represented in quatrains and seven-character ancient poems. Though existed before, these two forms of poetry became the pride of the poetry circle in the hands of the Tang people. Quatrains develop from folk songs; although the shortest, they have a more pure language compared with five-character ancient poems inevitably with more prose elements; the poems the Tang people have been singing are mainly quatrains, indicating that their characteristics of spontaneous flow of emotions are integrated with the language of life; it often "makes a breakthrough at one point but develops into a comprehensive one", reflecting a strong leaping, and "the abundance and freedom of the leaping nature" are beneficial to "the richness of poetic lyricism". Seven-character ancient poetry was a kind of new chanting poetry popular since the Sui and Tang Dynasties. It's different from five-character ancient poetry because the first half of the latter still has the rhythmic nature of four-character poetry, and is still used to long-term transitional expressions. However, seven-character ancient poetry has a brand-new three-character rhythm, and frequent change of rhymes in the Tang people's hands. Thus, "the sweeping changes and coherent style make the seven-character ancient form the most personalised and liberating" (115). The unique path of "singing" of seven-character ancient poetry and quatrains "shows that poetry was really liberated from the aristocratic parallelism of the Six Dynasties (220–589) and returned to the simple and natural language" (221). Led by them, regulated poems also stand out from long regulated poems along the path of simplicity and plainness. They are much more refined and flexible than long regulated poems, which is exactly in line with the characteristics of quatrains and seven-character ancient poems. All these suggest that

29 Ibid., 205.
30 Ibid., 210.

xxvi *Foreword to the Chinese edition*

"the peak of the whole poetry circle is based on the spontaneous flow of emotions in quatrains and seven-character ancient poems" (63). And the most outstanding works in the unique "frontier fortress poems" happen to be seven-character quatrains and seven-character ancient poems. After the Mid-Tang, the poetry circle had the differentiation of "plain and easy" and "hard and difficult". Profundity and simplicity were combined and flew towards ci poems (159–160). Lin Geng's elucidation not only more clearly presented the linguistic model of profundity out of simplicity of the Tang poetry, but highlighted the creative historical achievements of the Tang people.

Lin Geng's study of poeticisation focused on "the general language level at a time"; thus he did not confine himself to specific writers and works, but assessed the general situation of the whole poetry circle and even the literary circle. Before the Tang Dynasty, the process of poeticisation swept through the literary circles of the Wei, Jin, and Six Dynasties for about 400 years. In this period, proses and *fu* (also poetic exposition, rhapsody) gradually became similar to poetry in the process of poeticisation. *Fu* in this period broke away from the track of Han *fu*, and almost all their content and language "were developing around poetry as the centre" (89). The poeticisation of prose was highlighted in the unprecedented and unmatched *pianwen* (also parallel prose) of the Six Dynasties. Though flourishing in the Six Dynasties, *pianwen* declined and disappeared like *fu* in the Tang Dynasty when the poeticisation was mature. This shows that the predominance of *pianwen* is "a great wave around the rapid development of the poetic language, ebbing after the completion of poeticisation" (89). In this way, genres like prose, *fu*, and poetry were no longer genres unrelated to each other, but contained the in-depth evolution message of the literary language in their ups and downs. The commanding of the overall development of artistic language from a macroscopic and comprehensive perspective while breaking the stylistic boundaries was rare in previous studies. Thus, the literature of the Six Dynasties, which was simply denounced as "flowery" that people cherish not from the perspective of the traditional orthodox literary theory, regained new significance. As Lin Geng said, "The development of poetic language from the Jian'an era to the Sui Dynasty (581–618) paved the way for the Tang poetry, as the steepest Three Gorges helps the Yangtze River vigorously rush down a thousand li" (94). It shows his deep and keen sense of history to grasp the development of poetry. Of course, the Six Dynasties were still "at the stage of deliberate poetic pursuit" while "the traces of skills still existed", and the full maturity of language was yet to be achieved. However, in his discussion, Lin Geng not only reasonably explained many unique literary phenomena in the Six Dynasties, but traced the historical context of the Tang poetry that made it a high peak rather than a lonely peak, and thus it is significant and inspiring for future researchers.

The confluence of the maturity of poetic language and the maturity of the Tang society produced the peak of the Tang poetry, and created the ideal of

Foreword to the Chinese edition   xxvii

ancient Chinese poetry: "it is distinct, open-hearted, simple but profound; the vivid images, rich imagination, and abundant feelings are united into rich and endless expressions with ideological and artistic achievements. This is also known as the 'dense' style of the High Tang Atmosphere" (53). Why did the Tang poetry become the peak in the country of poetry? What lay behind its prosperity? Many scholars have been searching for answers, but only Lin Geng has answered this difficult question based on the integration of the life content, spiritual outlook, and high maturity of poetic language in the Tang Dynasty. Especially, he made a convincing exposition on how the poetic language matured through a long poeticisation process, thus having thoroughly explained the reasons leading to the prosperity of the Tang poetry from the perspective of poetics.

For nearly a century, new poetry has always been facing the pressure of fighting on two fronts. On the one hand, it must resolutely undermine the position of classical Chinese poetry, and be highly vigilant against the return of old poetry; on the other hand, it must learn from the modernisation experience of world literature, and, at the same time, guard against the denial and disregard of the tradition with a "Complete Westernisation". Lin Geng transformed such a sense of pressure and adversity into his own writing practice and theoretical thinking on new poetry, and then extended it for his inner drive of academic research on the poetic tradition. Inheritance, reference, and creation are not only the themes of Lin Geng's new poetry writing career featured by "asking for directions", but the centre of his diligent academic career. They contain a conscious sense of mission and lasting confidence in the construction of new poetry, and a keen aspiration for the prosperity of new poetry. It is this far-sighted approach of establishing the new from the old that makes Lin Geng's study of the history of poetry go beyond ordinary "academics" and become more distinct in contemporaneity, innovation, and originality. When his theory came out, it always aroused great concern and heated discussion in the academic circle.

Since the May Fourth Movement, the creative transformation of tradition has become an unavoidable and serious issue in the ideological, cultural, and academic circles. If we agree that "the genuine creativity and originality can only be obtained in the tradition of creativeness",[31] then Lin Geng's academic significance lies in his creativeness. It is beyond doubt that his achievements will continuously enlighten future generations with varying originality.

---

31 Lin Yusheng. *Creative Transformation of Chinese Tradition*, SDX Joint Publishing Company, 1988, 193.

Translator's notes

A Comprehensive Study of Tang Poetry is translated from a wide-reaching and creative Chinese masterpiece on the Tang poetry in the Golden Age of Chinese poetry (618–907). The first Chinese edition was published in 1987. In 2011, it was selected into the Masterpieces of Chinese Modern Academic Series and published by the Commercial Press with the support of the National Publication Fund.

Focusing on the poetic language, metrical patterns, landscape poetry, frontier fortress poetry, and the four greatest poets Li Bai, Du Fu, Wang Wei, and Bai Juyi, it has in-depth and refreshing discussions about the Jian'an Spirit, the High Tang Atmosphere, the Youth Spirit, maturity symbols, poeticisation, poetic vitality and new poetic prototypes with thousands of classical Tang poems themed in the love and friendship, aspirations and seclusion as well as travelling and home thoughts of people from all walks of life in that period when ancient China was the most civilised country in the world.

The original book includes three parts. The first part, "the Peak of the Tang Poetry", is particularly relevant to the book title; the second part, "Far Notes of the Tang Poetry", is related to the literature before the Tang Dynasty, many of which have little to do with the Tang poetry, or only have distant relationship and influence; the third part, "Essays on Poems", contains the literature of the Song Dynasty.

According to the opinion of the reviewers for the Chinese Fund for the Humanities and Social Sciences that the content should match the book title, I translated the preface "Why Do I Particularly Love the Tang Poetry", the "postscript", "Mr Lin Geng's Academic Chronology", and the foreword Zhong Yuankai's "Lin Geng's Poetic Thoughts and Academic Contributions". Moreover, the first part, "the Peak of the Tang Poetry" totalling 265 pages, was fully translated, with seven essays on the Tang poetry covering 17 pages in the third part. The translation was divided into two volumes with necessary editing and emendation.

As a matter of fact, Mr Lin Geng is highly accomplished in fields such as literature, philosophy, and poetry. Regarding poetry research, he is an expert not only in the Tang poetry, but in *Chuci*. A small number of essays that were not translated in this book should have opportunities to be translated in other monographs.

This year coincides with the 110th anniversary of Mr Lin Geng's birth. Our translation project team members sincerely wish that his academic thoughts would be disseminated around the world and have great influences on generations to come!

Finally, I would like to express my heartfelt gratitude to Prof. Kelly Washbourne at Kent State University for his meticulous editing of the manuscript, to Prof. Ni Chuanbin at Nanjing Normal University, to Prof. Yang Junfeng at Jilin International Studies University, to Prof. Liu Junping at Wuhan University, to Prof. Xu Mingwu at Huazhong University of Science and Technology, and to Prof. Tian Chuanmao, Prof. Xi Chuanjin, Prof. Tan Honghui, and Associate Prof. Ma Yan at Yangtze University for their constant support of this national translation project.

All mistakes are mine and mine alone.

Wang Feng
Yangtze University
June 2020

1 Chen Zi'ang and the Jian'an Spirit

The romantic tradition in ancient Chinese poetry

In recent studies on literary history, the status and roles of romanticism have become more adequately understood. Moreover, it is clear that the strong will of the people is conducive to the peak of literature and art, which is naturally favourable for romanticism. As the former Russian writer Maxim Gorky (1868–1936) says, romanticism and realism are two basic literary trends, while the former, known as "the eternal flame", first "strengthens people's will of life". Thus, the peak of romanticism in the High Tang poetry has a realistic foundation. Then, as a great poet at the eve of the High Tang, does Chen Zi'ang advocate romanticism or realism in his poetry writing and proposition? Of course, some romantic writers' works are not free from realistic elements; what we consider here is their principal preference.

An era with the majority of the population contributing to or supporting literature and art is rarely seen in history. However, it shows that the economic and political development meets and sustains the will of the people, which refers to the general public, or the majority of all the people, not necessarily including every single person at that time. Obviously, those corrupt officials and reactionary forces would never have the same goals as the general public. The High Tang appeared after defeating the Guanlong Bloc that had long been seizing political power. Obviously, the will of the Guanlong Bloc is not strong; however, that of the general public is strong, thus called the "will of the people". People are the masters pushing forward historical development. Since history at that time is not stagnant but developing, it conforms to the people's will to a certain extent. The will of the people is thus a liberating concept, which is conducive to the emergence of peak literature and art. The trend of realism in the Tang Dynasty appeared in the Zhenyuan (785–805), and Yuanhe (806–820) era expecting "a revival", not in the waning Late Tang. Is it not related to the strong will of people in the High Tang? Of course, a will or an ideal will always encounter contradictions. When the contradictions are simple and solvable, romanticism will prevail; when the contradictions are complicated and difficult to solve, it is more likely to bring about realism. Thus, the former is vigorous, and the latter is more observable. Of course, the two contradictions are often interlaced and combined in different degrees. Then, in what kind of historical conditions did Chen Zi'ang appear? This is the first issue to be discussed here.

2   *Chen Zi'ang and the Jian'an Spirit*

Chen Zi'ang carried on the Jian'an Spirit and enlightened the High Tang. What kind of era is Jian'an? What is the nature of the Jian'an Spirit? These were briefly mentioned in previous articles; however, these were not discussed in detail. Especially the Jian'an Spirit has always been interpreted differently, causing disagreement in understanding Chen Zi'ang, which is the second issue to be discussed.

The studies of Chen Zi'ang should focus on his poetry writing and poetic viewpoints. His times and his inheritance must be finally integrated with his thoughts, theories, and practice. This is the central issue for discussion. However, limited by the subject and scope, it is still mainly concerned with his relationship with the Jian'an Spirit.

Either Chen Zi'ang or the Jian'an Spirit will involve romanticism or realism, which are two basic tendencies or two creative approaches widely accepted in literary history. However, which one does Chen Zi'ang's body of work belong to? Inevitably, it also involves such issues as the creative approaches and style characteristics of classical Chinese poetry, especially lyrical poetry, which is another issue for further discussion.

All of these issues are complicated for me, yet restricted by time, I may have neglected something or made a few mistakes. I sincerely accept criticism and suggestions from readers around the world.

I The Wu Zetian era

The Wu Zetian (624–705) era is not considered an auspicious one as the spiritual outlook of the time under ancient historical conditions was overshadowed. The usurpations in the Jian'an era and the Wu Zetian era have long been criticised in feudal orthodox thinking; the "Usurpations of Wu and Wei" in history basically shows a negative attitude towards the latter era. Of course, when usurpation occurs, there are always brutal killings within the ruling class, which undoubtedly cast a negative shadow, as in the Jian'an era and the Wu Zetian era. Wu Zetian and Cao Cao (155–220) have different weaknesses in that Wu is an empress, which is regarded in Chinese tradition as "the hen crows in the morning", "the earth is above the heaven", or "the feminine is stronger than the masculine", deepening the subversive treachery; objectively, such an unstable factor under this historical condition is not conducive to unity. Cao Cao only inherited a crumbling mess of the Eastern Han Dynasty (25–220). At that time, the economy of northern China was not able to unify the divided country, showing that Cao Cao was in a worse position than Wu Zetian. Therefore, both eras could not become peaceful and unified auspicious times. Coincidentally, in the general impression, Cao Cao in iconography seems to have an innocent white face, while Wu Zetian is a wicked dark image for a long time. By comparing the two rulers in this way, I do not mean that they should have the same historical evaluation, nor is it a reverse of the verdict of Wu Zetian following that of Cao Cao. However, when Chen Zi'ang and the Jian'an Spirit (or the

Jian'an Air and Bone) are concerned, it is impossible to discuss the two eras without their main figures. In fact, no matter whether it is about Cao Cao or Wu Zetian, the historians' evaluation has always been different from the public perception.

First of all, historians almost unanimously believe that the Tang Dynasty from the Zhenguan era (627–649) to the Kaiyuan era (713–741) lasting for over 100 years developed in all aspects of economy, politics, and culture, which naturally includes the Wu Zetian era. In fact, there were only three decisive eras in the 138 years (618–755) from the founding of the Tang Dynasty to the An Shi Rebellion. First, it is the era of Emperor Taizong of Tang totalling 32 (618–649) years including the 23 years in Zhenguan, and the nine years of Wude (618–626) when he had actual control of the political power. The second is the Wu Zetian era lasting for 46 years from 660, the fifth year of the Xianqing period (656–661) when she officially began to administer state affairs, until 705, the first year of the Shenlong period (705–707) when she abdicated the throne. If counted from the year when she was appointed the empress consort in the sixth year of the Yonghui period (650–655), she had been in power for 51 years (665–705)—a little more than half a century. The third is the Kaiyuan era of Emperor Xuanzong (685–762) of Tang, which lasts for a total of 43 years (713–755). These three eras account for 126 years of the total 138 years. This is the period of the developing times lasting over 100 years before the An Shi Rebellion. The Wu Zetian era was the longest between the two other eras. If Wu Zetian's era of 51 years is not rising but stagnant, then why would historians say that in more than a hundred years it has been rising? The Zhenguan era is well governed, and the Kaiyuan era is auspicious. If the Wu Zetian era between them were chaotic and disastrous, how can we explain such a historical anomaly? The Prosperity of Zhenguan lasted for only 20 years. If it hit the submerged reef of the Wu Zetian era of 51 years, would it have been cut in half and collapsed completely? How could the Prosperity of Zhenguan exist? If Kaiyuan had not prospered, then there would not have been more than 100 years of development. Therefore, historians have always been affirming the success of the Wu Zetian era with specific details. Here is an excerpt from Prof. Shang Yue's *Outline of Chinese History*:

> In the Early Tang (618–712), the Guanlong group supported Li Yuan and his sons to found the Tang Dynasty and became the most powerful force. Emperor Taizong had *The Clan Chronicle* critically revised to "make the heroes of the world participate in my reign," giving a certain blow to the powerful clans and landlords... Wu Zetian first administered state affairs with political reforms, then dethroned Emperor Zhongzong and Emperor Ruizhong, and then changed the name of the dynasty into Zhou (690–705) and became the empress regnant. [She] developed the imperial examination system by paying special attention to the examination of *Jinshi* (successful test-takers in the imperial examination),

4 *Chen Zi'ang and the Jian'an Spirit*

and opened a convenient door for scholar-bureaucrats in Shandong and Jiangnan (also the River South) to participate in the regime. The aristocratic Guanlong group was completely defeated even though they had had the political and economic privileges and monopolised the central government since the Western Wei Dynasty (535–556). Among the scholar-bureaucrats that succeeded in the imperial examinations, quite a few became "famous ministers" in feudal times such as Di Renjie, and Zhang Jianzhi, or "famous ministers in Kaiyuan" pre-selected for Emperor Xuanzong such as Yao Chong (also Yao Yuanzhi) and Song Jing.

During Wu Zetian's reign, the Tang Empire continued to develop. [She] developed the imperial examination system inside, resisted the outside disturbance of Turks, Turpan and Khitan, and further built the passage to the Western Regions, playing a positive role in the social and economic development in some aspects. Needless to say, some of Wu Zetian's measures, such as excessive constructions, heavy taxes and frequent recruitment, and the appointment of cruel officials and her own clans like Wu Yizong, were harmful to the people.

In summary, Wu Zetian is the successor to the Prosperity of Zhenguan. She overthrew the aristocratic Guanlong group retaliating against them in the Zhenguan era, carried on the military frontier defence of Emperor Taizong, elected over 70 ministers leading to a political success similar to that in the Zhenguan era, and continued the social and economic development, although she had shortcomings, which should also be pointed out.

From the pre-selection of famous ministers in Kaiyuan for Emperor Xuanzong, Wu Zetian was not only a follower of the Zhenguan era but also a forerunner of the High Tang. Wu Zetian has a deep relationship with Yao Chong and Song Jing. Yao Chong, the first famous minister in the Kaiyuan era, is in fact only second to those few prime ministers in Wu Zetian's imperial court. One of the prime ministers Zhang Jianzhi was even recommended by him. However, the strangest fact is that Yao Chong participated in the battle led by Zhang Jianzhi against the other two Zhangs to welcome Emperor Zhongzong to the throne, which is recorded in chapter 24 of the *Comprehensive Mirror in Aid of Governance: Records of Tang*:

> When the Empress Dowager (Wu Zetian) was dethroned and banished to the Shangyang palace, only one of the prime ministers of husbandry Yao Chong sobbed and shed tears. Huan Yanfan and Zhang Jianzhi asked him, "Is it the right time for you to cry today? This might be the beginning of your misfortunes!" Yuanzhi said: "I served the empress regnant Zetian for long. Seeing her dethronement suddenly, I feel so sad and cannot help crying. Moreover, when I followed you to kill the treacherous officials, it's out of righteousness for the throne. Today when I bid farewell to the empress regnant, it's out of sympathy for the throne. Even convicted guilty, I cried with my heart".

Chen Zi'ang and the Jian'an Spirit 5

The deep relationship between Yao Chong and Wu Zetian is clearly seen. However, according to historical records, Yao Chong seems to live for political ideals rather than for fame and power, which shows the political stance of Wu Zetian. Song Jing is also an unusual character in Wu Zetian's imperial court. *New Stories of the Great Tang* records that

> Song Jing was assigned to be the County Judge of Yangzhou because the imperial court could not tolerate him for his frequent discussions of its gains and losses, while in fear of his impartiality. Then he reported, "Though talentless, I reside in the Supervisory Institution. However, a County Judge is a lower-rank inspector in a prefecture or county. I do not know the intention of the order, nor the reason; thus, I plead not to accept it". After a short time, he was ordered to interrogate Qutu Zhongxiang, the Commander of Youzhou, but Jing refused again, saying "A Mid-Imperial Supervisor should not go out for such a mission if it is not an important military affair. And Zhongxiang is accused of bribery, which is governed by higher officials like the imperial inspectors and lower officials like the prefecture inspectors. I am afraid the current mission is not out of Your Majesty's intention. As that might endanger me, please allow me to disobey such an order". After a month, the Deputy Supervisor Li Qiao was ordered to the Shu region. He was happy to invite Jing and said, "Having received such a grace, I want to show my gratitude with you". Jing said, "Grace is shown with etiquette, but I am not shown any etiquette. I should not go with you, nor should I show my gratitude". Then he reported, "I am the only supervisor. I don't understand why Your Majesty ordered Qiao the Deputy to Shu as there are no important affairs in either the Long or Shu regions. In fear of failing the tasks in the imperial court, I plead not to accept it".

Vile officials tried every possible means to drive Song Jing out of the imperial court, but they failed. Why? And the repeated "plead not to accept it" forms a unique style in the Zhenguan era. If Empress Wu and Song Jing did not deeply understand each other, such pleadings would be unthinkable in feudal times.

The above two examples of the famous ministers in Kaiyuan illustrate the close relationship between the Wu Zetian era and the Kaiyuan era. In the rapid rise and development of over 100 years, the Wu Zetian era serves as an important link between past and future. Thus, this era has more essential characteristics though it is overshadowed. In terms of social development, when feudalism takes the place of slavery, it does not immediately become a backward system. In its early years, feudalism must struggle to get rid of the remnants of slavery in order to move forward productively. Many historians at home and abroad even think that the Han Dynasty still has a slavery system, which shows the deep-seatedness of the slavery remnants. Feudal society therefore often stagnates even in its progressive stage, and the main base

6 *Chen Zi'ang and the Jian'an Spirit*

of the slavery remnants is bound in the feudal aristocratic group, which is a privileged monopoly class, or a super exploiting class; the development and stagnation at the progressive stage of the feudal society often depend on the growth or decline of this class, i.e., is it suppressed or connived? In the early stage of feudal society, the peasant uprisings were also aimed at fighting against this class. If enlightened emperors wanted to give in to the peasants, they must first suppress this aristocratic class. Cao Cao, Emperor Taizong, and Wu Zetian were the same in many aspects. Is this not an essential issue? Wu Zetian's cruelty due to her own political weakness should be criticised. However, historical records show that Wu Zetian's appointment of cruel officials was mainly aimed at the "hundred officials" within the ruling class, rather than the ordinary people. In appointing cruel officials, Wu also used many famous officials such as Yao Chong, Xu Yougong, Li Zhaode, Li Rizhi, and Yan Shansi to constrain those cruel officials at the same time. Wu Zetian is similar to Cao Cao in the appreciation of punishment, killing, power, and sophisticated tactics. Chapter 21 of the *Comprehensive Mirror in Aid of Governance: Records of Tang* records:

> When people recommended by officials were introduced to the Empress Dowager, she would promote all of them, not asking whether they are wise or foolish. People wrote a poem about it, saying "Instructors loaded in carriages, / Imperial censors are grains in tanks. / Imperial inspectors plenty, / Revisers are modelled out of bowels". At that time, Shen Quan-jiao, a *Juren* (a successful candidate in the imperial examinations at the provincial level), added to the saying, "Muddle-hearted are inspectors / As the Saint Empress is thoughtless". Imperial Supervisor Ji Xianzhi arrested him and impeached him for his slander of the imperial court. Ji pleaded to have him hit with a big stick in the court and killed later. The Empress Dowager smiled and said, "If you have not overdone it, why should you worry about others' words. You should release him". Hearing this, Xianzhi was ashamed. The Empress Dowager received the hearts of the country by providing numerous positions with a good allowance. However, those who were not up to the requirement of the post were displaced, punished, or even prisoned and killed. Thus, with the rule of reward and punishment, the Empress Dowager administered the country by proposing and implementing policies with observation and judgement. Thus, heroes and talents rushed to serve the court.

When Cao Cao wanted to suppress the aristocracy, he gave orders of "seeking talents" or "seeking exceptionally gifted people". Wu Zetian also took similar measures such as the Imperial Examination System to crack down on the Guanlong group. Cao Cao was progressive in these measures, and so was Wu Zetian. This is a kind of quality more intrinsic than the shadow on the surface. The Kaiyuan era inherited this more intrinsic quality, and developed further; a series of weaknesses such as the usurpation and the ruling of an empress regnant disappeared, thus clearing away the dark shadow from the Wu Zetian era. There emerged an uncorrupted, stable, and a unified golden age; and the Wu Zetian era was just its prelude. This was the eve of an era of vigorous national will and a rising era of deep romantic temperament, witnessing the appearance of Chen Zi'ang.

II The Jian'an Spirit

The issue of the Jian'an Spirit can be divided into two parts. The first is the original meaning of the Jian'an Spirit, and how to understand it in the traditional sense; as an ancient poet, Chen Zi'ang can only have a traditional understanding of it according to its original meaning, then is this traditional understanding romantic or realistic? The second part is on whether the concept of the Jian'an Spirit can represent the main tendency of the Jian'an poetry; what are the main tendencies of the Jian'an poetry? What is its essence? Does it conform to the traditional understanding of the Jian'an Spirit? I think these are the central issues of the Jian'an Spirit.

Let's start with its original meaning. It first appeared in *Poetry Appreciation* as "the Jian'an Strength" (or "the Jian'an Air and Strength"). In opposition to the dispiritedness in the Qi (479–502) and Liang (502–557) Dynasties, Zhong Rong advocated learning from the Jian'an era and put forward this challenging slogan. This slogan was never explained in any other way but appeared as a bright and vigorous style. *The Literary Mind and the Carving of Dragons*: *Spirit* states:

> Sima Xiangru has written a *fu* about an immortal with sky-soaring spirit. He is considered a true master of *fu* because of his powerful strength.

Although *The Literary Mind and the Carving of Dragons* is not limited to poetry and the Jian'an tradition, "sky-soaring spirit" and "powerful strength" are concepts obviously the same as those in *Poetry Appreciation*. In *The Literary Mind and the Carving of Dragons*, "strength" is related to the wind, which is identical to the air, as in expressions such as "When the air of the writing is cool, the style of writing is clear", and "If it lacks the air, then the style is not established". This is similar to "Love to be unusual with the air; variate the air to be extraordinary" in *Poetry Appreciation*. This is also a far-sighted romantic style. Scholars always believe that romanticism focuses on feelings, and *The Literary Mind and the Carving of Dragons* also states, "The expression of touching feelings must begin with the air". However, the use of "strength" to mark the style of Jian'an in *Poetry Appreciation* is to illustrate a positive romantic characteristic. *Poetry Appreciation* also remarks, "Make it strong with the strength; enrich it with colourful ornaments", showing that the strength plays a key role in the style of poetry. Rhetoric is also related to the literary style, but it is secondary and ornamental; while the bright

8 *Chen Zi'ang and the Jian'an Spirit*

and powerful style as the backbone shows a characteristic quality, which is called the air, and sometimes called the bone in *Poetry Appreciation*. For example, "the bone and the air are extremely high; the words and expressions are colourful". "The bone and the air is extremely high" is similar to "Make it strong with the strength", while "the words and expressions are colourful" resembles "enrich it with colourful ornaments". It is also said that "the real bone endures the frost; the high wind is beyond conventions". Thus, the later generation called the Jian'an Strength as the Jian'an Spirit (or the Jian'an Air and Bone). It shows that the essence of romanticism is far-sighted, ideal, heroic, and different from the conventional, which are the original meaning and traditional understanding of the Jian'an Spirit. Li Bai says:

> Your Penglai writing has the Jian'an Bone
> And in the middle a touch of Xie's freshness.
> All of us have vigorous thought endless,
> Almost near the sky to touch the bright moon.

The "Jian'an Bone" here is "vigorous", "endless", "near the sky", and "to touch the bright moon". Can these not belong to romanticism? This is what is called the "sky-soaring spirit" in *The Literary Mind and the Carving of Dragons*. The "Jian'an Bone", "the Jian'an Spirit", and "the Jian'an Strength", therefore, are the same, that is, the spiritual essence and style of romanticism. As for the "bone" mentioned in *The Literary Mind and the Carving of Dragons: Spirit*, it is close to a practice of polishing words and sentences, as shown in "A writer who knows the bone of an article must have a good choice of words", "Key words are formal and straightforward", and "Polishing words steadfast and making it irreplaceable". This kind of refined accomplishment, the "ability to be clear", also belongs to the category of style, and conforms to "the Strength", but in *The Literary Mind and the Carving of Dragons*, it is a different conception related to the spiritual essence. It is complementary to the Jian'an Spirit, but they are not the same, as is said in "Pan Xu wrote about the King of Wei, imitating the classics. It made other talents stop writing because the bone of his writing is superb". It has gone far beyond the scope of literature, involving a much wider range than general rhetoric and expressions, which will not be discussed in detail in this book.

Scholars hold the same view on the spirit of the Jian'an poetry, which is concluded in *The Literary Mind and the Carving of Dragons* as: "Be open-minded to show their air; be open-hearted to present their talents". What creative approaches have the characteristics of "open-minded", "show their air", "open-hearted", and "present their talents"? This is self-evident. In his "Thirty Poems on Poetry", Yuan Haowen says,

> Cao and Liu are seated, roaring like giant tigers.
> Who in the Four Oceans can duel with the two?

Pitiful that Liu Yueshi, the Bingzhou governor
Holding a spear, wasn't among the Jian'an group.

"Cao and Liu are two saints of writing", which has been stated in *Poetry Appreciation*. However, Yuan Haowen pointed out more clearly the characteristics of heroic personality. Moreover, he thought that a poet with a heroic spirit like Liu Kun (also Liu Yueshi) should make his fame in the Jian'an poetry. So what creation method involves personal character to such a degree? This is also self-evident. The characteristics of romanticism marked by the Jian'an Spirit have always been the representative style of the Jian'an poetry.

Jian'an is an epoch-making era born out of peasant uprisings. So what kind of social development did the peasant uprisings promote? What on earth did it bring to the people? Some scholars believe that the peasant uprisings in the Jian'an era mainly brought about wars, which cannot answer the question, because wars are clearly harmful to production, bringing sufferings and calamity to the people. Is it the effect of peasant uprisings? Wars are only means for a higher purpose; they are necessary, and sometimes have inevitable side effects in the pursuit of a primary aim. The historical development must go through specific historical stages, and it's impossible to achieve that overnight. If it wants to get out of feudalism, the society must first develop the feudal society, especially when the social system is still in a rising stage; when there is no more progressive social system in the world at that time, it would be impossible to get out of it without the development of this system. This is quite obvious. The peasant uprisings pushed forward the historical development, not because it brought about wars, but because it broke the stagnant state of the feudal society at a certain period of time, suppressed the powerful forces hindering the development of the feudal society, educated the ruling class at that time, and liberated the progressive forces of society; thus, liberal political rulers began to make concessions to the people and ensured the development of productivity. However, productivity is never developed out of exploitation or suppression. On the contrary, it develops only when the enthusiasm of the working class is raised. The reason why slavery evolves into feudalism has illustrated this truth. The peasant uprisings in the Jian'an era mainly brought about development rather than wars. Literature reflects the spiritual outlook of that era, and thus it is mainly about the inspiring role rather than the side effects. Of course, since wars are objective reality, they should be reflected in literature, directly or indirectly. As the Jian'an Spirit is born in the ruins of wars, it must reflect on them. *The Literary Mind and the Carving of Dragons: Times Change* states,

> With pens, contenting songs are composed; with ink, conversations and derisions become compositions. Writings at that time are usually open-minded; mostly originated from long-time wars and exiles, declining customs and resentful practices, reflecting their profound aspiration and prolific writings; thus, they are broad-minded with various spirits.

10 *Chen Zi'ang and the Jian'an Spirit*

However, it cannot be said that this style has no reflections on wars. That is why Liu Kun, who engaged in the wars, should be one of the Jian'an poets. But this is not the main aspect after all. Only a few works in the Jian'an literature were directly concerned with the wars, which only appeared in the early Jian'an era. After the Battle of Chibi, the three kingdoms of Wei, Shu, and Wu were basically in a relatively stable situation to restore production. Thus, wars cannot represent the whole Jian'an era. Throughout Jian'an the far-reaching struggles persisted, as did the desire to further promote the historical development of the stagnant feudal society from the Han Dynasty on. They are the main reasons behind and strength of the Jian'an Spirit, which is "usually open-minded", and "broad-minded with various spirits". The far-sighted romanticism is to strengthen the will to life, which is called the Jian'an Spirit, the most representative style of the Jian'an era.

From Qu Yuan to Li Bai, the excellent tradition of romanticism in Chinese poetry has always concentrated on the reflection of political struggles. The spirit of patriotism, the quality of resisting power and aristocracy, and the enlightened political ideal of recommending the virtuous and capable have become the central themes of poetry in the development of Chinese feudal society; the Jian'an Spirit has added glory to this tradition. This is the reason why Chen Zi'ang highly advocates the spirit.

III Chen Zi'ang's poetic viewpoints

Chen Zi'ang's poetic viewpoints are mainly shown in his preface to "On Long Bamboos". This preface says:

> In the past five hundred years, the way of writing always has drawbacks. The spirit of the Han and Wei Dynasties has not been passed down to the Jin (266–420) and Song of the Southern (also Liu Song, 420–479) Dynasties, even though there is evidence of relevant literature. I observed the poetry between the Qi and Liang Dynasties at leisure times and sighed that they were colourful and ornamental, but without metaphorical writing for profound thinking or feelings. I thought about those ancient people and was often afraid of being indirect and dispirited. I was troubled by the incapability of spirited and elegant writing. But yesterday I saw "Chanting of the Lone Phoenix Tree" by Lord Ming (also Dongfang Qiu) at the home of my friend Xie San. It is characterised by a dignified and serene spirit, touching emotions, clarity and conciseness, and the refined musicality with the clankings of metal and stone. Thus, I changed my mind and was not worried any more. I never expected that the most classical writing could be seen in this writing, which can make the Jian'an authors smile at each other with understanding.

In this preface there are two motifs: one is "metaphorical writing", and the other is "spirit". "Metaphorical writing" means it should establish a metaphorical relationship with politics, while "spirit" refers to the Jian'an Spirit. Chen Zi'ang thinks that the tradition of the Jian'an Spirit can still be seen in the poems of Ruan Ji (also Ruan Sizong, 210–263) from the Wei Dynasty (220–265) in expressing his feelings, so it is also called the "Han and Wei Spirit". This is also in line with the original meaning in *Poetry Appreciation*, which believes that after Liu Kun and Guo Pu, the Jian'an Spirit has disappeared. But Chen Zi'ang says, "The Han and Wei Spirit is not passed down to the Jin and Song of the Southern Dynasties". However, the meanings are exactly the same. Although "classical writing" and "the Jian'an Spirit" are different, they share similarities. Chen Zi'ang focused on their same origin from Jian'an, and adopted the concept of "spirit". What's more, Chen Zi'ang adopted the Han and Wei Spirit because the Han and Wei Dynasties include the Jian'an era. When he mentioned the "classical writing", he also thought that it is with "a dignified and serene spirit, touching emotions, clarity and conciseness, and the refined musicality with the clankings of metal and stone". This "spirit" is synonymous with the "strength", and the "touching emotions, clarity and conciseness, and the refined musicality" are obviously traditional characteristics of the vigorous and open-hearted style of the Jian'an Spirit, so it can "make the Jian'an authors smile at each other with understanding". However, the most powerful and specific explanation about Chen Zi'ang's poetic viewpoints is "On Long Bamboos", which is a mutual test of Chen Zi'ang's theory and practice. Now the whole poem is introduced below. It is almost self-evident whether it is realistic or romantic.

> Dragon bamboos the South Mount by
> Are lone, slim, green with gracefulness.
> They climb up to the summit high;
> In drizzle, they grow down in darkness.
> Many flying squirrels squeak at night;
> The spring is noisy in the day.
> After the spring breeze fades away,
> There comes the clear and cold dew white.
> Their sad sound, a harsh metallic din.
> Their dense colour to jade is akin.
> In the cold years with frost and snow,
> Hiding colours, only green they show.
> They hate not freezing weather, true?
> With spring woods, they are shy to vie.
> Spring woods now more decayed they grew.
> The bamboos never wither and die.
> Like metal and stone, they wish to
> Stay faithful forever and aye.

12　*Chen Zi'ang and the Jian'an Spirit*

> Ling Lun a musician makes them
> Flutes to follow the phoenix's rhythm.
> They and zithers to the clouds fly
> And play music in the Heaven high.
> Wonderful songs are ever-changing;
> They play "The Royal Flutes" nine times.
> For the musician's carving,
> They would serve the fairies oftentimes.
> In a dragon chariot green,
> The Purple-Bird pipes are in dismay.
> With a Chinese Faerie Queen,
> "Rising to Heaven" is what they play.
> Hand in hand, they reach the white sun.
> Far in the Red town, they have great fun.
> Gently, humbly, red-crowned cranes dance
> In colourful clouds of romance.
> With immortals ever, they would stay
> In three peaks till the Capital Jade.

In this poem, the long bamboos are metaphorised to show the poet's ideals. Through rich imagination, it portrays the image of "clarity and conciseness". This shows the ideal and singing of a lofty quality in political struggles since the great romantic poet Qu Yuan's "Ode to the Orange" showing his aloofness from politics and material pursuits. This is what's called the "metaphorical writing". In "Li Sao" (also "Encountering Sorrow"), Qu Yuan uses a great number of fragrant grasses to metaphorically unveil his ideal. Afterwards, the poet Zhang Jiuling's "Thoughts" has "In the River South, the red orange grows", "Aromatic grass flourishes in spring", "Why does the lone parasol tree grow", etc. These poems can well explain the origin and development of this tradition. From here we can also imagine what kind of poem "The Lone Phoenix Tree" by Dongfang Qiu is. As for "On Long Bamboos", this poem concretely shows how similar it is in style and content to the "Three Poems for My Cousin" by Liu Zhen, who is one of the typical representative poets of the Jian'an Spirit. The most outstanding of the three poems is the second:

> Graceful are pines on the mountain;
> Wild is the wind in the valley.
> How strong the sound of the wind is!
> How powerful pine branches are!
> The ice-frost is miserable,
> But the pines are always upright.
> Not suffering from the freezing cold?
> Pine and cypress have their nature.

This is a work that "Loves to be unusual with the air; variates the air to be extraordinary", showing that "the true bone fears not the frost; the superior style is beyond conventions". Moreover, is this not exactly what appears in "On Long Bamboos"?

> Dragon bamboos the South Mount by
> Are lone, slim, green with gracefulness.
> In the cold years with frost and snow,
> Hiding colours, only green they show.
> They hate not freezing weather, true?
> With spring woods, they are shy to vie.
> Spring woods now more decayed they grew.
> The bamboos never wither and die.

Even the ways of expression are so similar that I do not think there is much to say here. And if we cite Liu Zhen's third poem, it will be more interesting. The lone bamboo was also metaphorised in the poem:

> Phoenixes meet in the South Mount
> And wander at bamboo roots lone.
> Their hearts are never complacent;
> They beat their wings for the purple zone.
> Do not they always fly up hard?
> Ashamed to crowd with sparrows unknown!
> When should the phoenixes come here?
> They come for saint men on the throne.

This actually resembles the latter part of "On Long Bamboos":

> Ling Lun a musician makes them
> Flutes to follow the phoenix's rhythm.
> ...
> Hand in hand, they reach the white sun.
> Far in the Red town, they have great fun.
> Gently, humbly, red-crowned cranes dance
> In colourful clouds of romance.
> With immortals ever, they would stay
> In three peaks till the Capital Jade.

One says, "Phoenixes meet in the South Mount", while the other says, "Flutes to follow the phoenix's rhythm". One says, "They beat their wings for the purple zone", while the other says, "Hand in hand, they reach the white sun". One says, "Ashamed to crowd with sparrows unknown", while the other says, "Gently, humbly, red-crowned cranes dance". One has an explicit theme: "When should the phoenixes come here? / They come for saint men on the throne". The other is more implicit with a pun in suggesting that "With immortals ever, they would stay / In three peaks till the Capital Jade". The "Capital Jade" refers to where the god of gods lives, and the capital of the human world at the same time. In short, we should look for the "Capital Jade", which requires the "men on the

14   *Chen Zi'ang and the Jian'an Spirit*

throne" to be "saint". I think it is difficult to explain the relationship between theory and practice if the idea of the preface to "On Long Bamboos" is not reflecting the ideal of the Jian'an Spirit. And whether the tradition of the Jian'an Spirit is romantic or realistic also has a more powerful evidence here.

IV Romantic spirit in Chen Zi'ang's poetry

Chen Zi'ang's "Thoughts" basically develop around the theme of "On Long Bamboos". Of course, in the trend of romanticism, there may also be elements of realism, as shown in some of Li Bai's "Ancient Style" (or *gufeng*) poems. In his 38 poems entitled "Thoughts", Chen Zi'ang also wrote down a few lines from reality such as "The sage is never self-serving" and "At dusk in the Year of the Pig". However, the central themes of these poems are the ambition to make contributions, the metaphorical political writing as shown in "On Long Bamboos", and the outspoken expression against the unfair hindrance of ideals. For example:

> Born in a noble family,
> I do love talents all my life.
> Thinking of rewarding the country,
> I play the sword in the grassy wild.
> I've been to the lone west fortress
> And the northern Tribe Chief terrace.
> Climbing to see a thousand *li*,
> I feel nostalgic about the past!
> Who says "Forget not the fortune ill"?
> It's been ground to ashes and dust!

— "Thoughts" No. 34

Such lofty ambitions even exist in seclusion poems, for example:

> I love Guiguzi, a strategist
> Who lives by a stream, clear and bright.
> Knowing all about governance,
> He hides himself among clouds white.
> Seven States just like dragons fight,
> But none rules the chaotic world.
> Fame, like floating clouds, has no worth.
> Better obey the time and write.
> Talents can spread in the universe,
> Or it can be concealed in a roll.
> Why admire the long life of mount woods?
> They only grow with elk herds in vain.

—"Thoughts" No. 11

Chen Zi'ang and the Jian'an Spirit 15

It shows that even if "He hides himself among clouds white", he would "Better obey the time and write". When the time comes, he would contribute "all about governance" and make them "spread in the universe". There are also works completely similar to "On Long Bamboos", as in:

Growing in spring and summer hours,
The orchid bears lush leaves so green.
The lonely but best colours are seen
On its purple stems and red flowers.
Slowly the white sun goes away,
And the autumn wind makes it sway.
When its life is shaken and past,
What has its aroma left at last?

—"Thoughts" No. 1

Metaphorical writing can also be seen. It also shows the injustice aroused in the pursuit of ideals, as shown in "I'm ill for long, living in woods", "When will I stop my plaintive sighs?", and "Why does no one show gratitude? / The present custom decays it!" Moreover,

To respect Minister Yue Yi,
The King of Yan would share his nation.
Lu Lian refused the dukedom of Qi;
Left his official seal for Handan.
All of them were gone forever;
For whom I sigh with such feelings!

—"Thoughts" No. 15

Isn't Li Bai active on paper? His heroic personality is shown in:

The northern wind blows the sea trees.
Bleak is the frontier in autumn.
Whose son by the pavilion is
Sad for the Moon Tower at home?
He said he was a guest from Youyan,
And travelled far after marriage.
He killed officials with red pellets,
And took vengeance with a white blade.
Avoiding foes, he went to the sea,
But was forced to serve in this state.
He is three thousand *li* from home;
The Liaoshui River is long and wide.
Angry for Hu soldiers' attacks,
While ashamed of the Han Dynasty.

16　*Chen Zi'ang and the Jian'an Spirit*

After seventy deadly fights, why
Isn't he a marquis, though white-haired!

— "Thoughts" No. 33

The swordsmen, frontier, ideals and injustice, and the images of "High trees have more sad wind" and "Bright moon shining on high towers" form a familiar style. There are also famous works besides "Thoughts", such as "King Zhao of the Yan":

Mounting south by the Monument Palace,
I looked at the Golden Terrace afar.
The hills are covered with tall trees.
But where is the King of Zhao, alas?
Now that his great empire has gone,
I have to ride on horseback!

And "Crown Prince of Yan":

The Qin Emperor was cruel,
Deepening Crown Prince Yan's hatred.
Once hearing Tian Guang's virtue,
He gave him a dagger and gold.
They failed to kill the emperor,
But sadness lasts a thousand years.

These poems of lofty ambition belong to a series of poems, "Visiting the Historical Jiqiu". A preface states:

In the Year of the Rooster, I made an expedition northward from Jimen, and visited the old capital of Yan. Its great city has vanished, and I could not help lamenting about it! I remembered that generals like Yue Yi and scholars like Zou Yan travelled here, so I mounted the Ji tower and composed seven poems to commemorate it.

However, it is another masterpiece rather than this series of poems that better expresses his magnificent ambition and open-hearted feeling of the injustice in this preface. That is the "Song of Mounting the Youzhou Terrace":

Before, no ancients were seen;
After, no followers will be seen.
How vast the sky and earth are;
Alone, I feel sad and shed tears.

This eternal masterpiece makes Chen Zi'ang's status unforgettable in the history of Chinese poetry. Its radiance, the eternal flame of romanticism, brightens up the poetry circle of the High Tang.

V "Song of Mounting the Youzhou Terrace" and its romantic creative approaches

The poem "Song of Mounting the Youzhou Terrace" enjoys such great fame and impresses people deeply. It is a supernova that stands out among other stars. However, it has only four short lines. Poetry theorists who require concrete elements feel that there is almost nothing specific here. However, nobody can deny the high value of this poem. This contradiction is long-standing. Nikolay Chernyshevsky's *Aesthetic Relations of Art to Reality* has very interesting and inspiring statements on poetry:

> Now let's talk about poetry, the most sublime and perfect art in all arts. The problems of poetry are concerned with all the theories of arts. In terms of content, poetry is far superior to other arts, and all other arts can tell us less than one per cent of what poetry tells us. But when we turn our attention to the power and vividness of the subjective impressions of poetry and other arts on human, this relationship changes completely. All other arts, like a living reality, act directly on our senses, while poetry acts on our imaginations.... Therefore, in terms of the power and clarity of subjective impression, poetry is not only far inferior to reality but far inferior to other arts.... The best and clearest figure depicted in poetry is still a general and fuzzy sketch without clear outlines ...

This passage can give us great inspiration: "Poetry" basically "acts on our imaginations" with a "fuzzy sketch without clear outlines". If that's true for those longer European poems, then it's truer for the shorter traditional Chinese lyric poems, which explains why the tradition of romanticism in ancient Chinese poetry is more prevalent and outstanding. And if we use the specific and realistic measurements in the realistic creative approaches that "like a living reality" to evaluate any poem created with the romantic creative approaches, it is bound to be vague and powerless. However, it cannot be denied that it is lofty and perfect. The contradiction is that such measurements are incorrect. When romanticism is still a vassal or tributary of realism, such measures may be justifiable in theory; however, when romanticism and realism are two creative approaches of similar importance, such measures are clearly inappropriate. Now, we have clarified this point.

The poem "Song of Mounting the Youzhou Terrace" by itself is a forceful proof of the power of the romantic creative approach while showing its characteristics. It is indeed acting on imaginations, and the outlines are unclear; however, it's sublime and perfect; and it objectively gives people an indelible impression and contains passionate and heartfelt power. With flesh and blood, it is not deprived of ideological content even if it might not be specific. The result of measuring everything in terms of specificity is to deny many excellent works in Chinese poetry over thousands of years, and to draw a wrong conclusion that "A dog's tail can be knit after the ferrets"

18   *Chen Zi'ang and the Jian'an Spirit*

is more poetic than the "Song of Mounting the Youzhou Terrace". It only hinders us from deeply understanding the excellent tradition of classical Chinese poetry. What is the clear specificity of the "Song of Mounting the Youzhou Terrace"? It's almost as if this ancient masterpiece is meant to directly converse with time and space through the whole infinite universe of endless loneliness. It is indeed difficult to define its outline or specificity; only the line "Alone, I feel sad and shed tears" is slightly more specific, just as the word "sad" in "High terraces have more sad wind". However, the outline is still unclear. What's more, "Before, no ancients were seen; / After, no followers will be seen" describes what is (not) seen after mounting the terrace. "How vast the sky and earth are; / Alone, I feel sad and shed tears" is similar to "more sad winds". It is not specific indeed. The question is, if there are no real and unusually profound feelings, is it possible to write down such a magnificent poem that stands out in the past millennium? This is a specific test for all theories. Therefore, Chen Zi'ang's "Song of Mounting the Youzhou Terrace" provides a powerful research clue for the romantic creative approach in ancient lyric poetry.

16 September 1959
Originally published in *Literature Review*, 1959 (5)

Answers to Readers' Questions

Dear Editors,
The letter and the attached comments by Mr Liang Chaoran were read. Below is my brief response:

First, the historical evaluation of the Wu Zetian era regarding its economy and politics, I think, should focus on the historical development by looking at the key issues from a comprehensive point of view rather than on a few facts. To judge whether this half a century is progressive or regressive, I believe, we should listen more to historians' opinions. The productivity of ancient feudal society was low, and no matter how prosperous the society was, drought, waterlogging, and pests could not be completely avoided. At that time, the crisscrossed frontier was fragile to frequent wars along the border, leading to unavoidable military and economic tensions and losses. The Wu Zetian era lasted for a little more than half a century. It is far from enough to justify the ups and downs by mentioning what happened in a certain region during this period. I myself am a layman in history, but most of my comments on this era are based on and complementary to historians' opinions.

Second, I wrote two articles on romanticism last year. In addition to "Chen Zi'ang and the Jian'an Spirit", I published in the *Poetry Journal* an article entitled "Ancient Style: When a Millet is Sown in Spring". In both articles, I explained from many aspects that the essence of romanticism is the ideals and expectations, and the resulting open-minded feelings of injustice. There seems to be no divergence of opinions. The difference is that I think this is a characteristic of the romantic spirit, while the romantic creative approach has other characteristics. Of course, creative approaches are rooted in the creative spirit, but they are not the same. Are ideals and feelings of injustice more concerned with the spirit or approaches? I still stand with the former.

Third, since romanticism is full of ideals and vision, more rapid and smooth development of the time will be more conducive to the development of this spirit. Of course, the "smooth development" is not without difficulties, but the progressive power is predominant in the development of contradictions; otherwise, it will not develop rapidly. In Chinese history, the pre-Qin Dynasty is a fast-developing era full of liberatory spirit, and the entire era is also full of romantic temperament. Thus, in the history of literature, there appeared Qu Yuan, the first great romantic poet. This is completely in line with the law of development. The war or stability is not the decisive yardstick for measuring the rapid development or stagnation of the time. The course of the victorious revolution undoubtedly experiences a time of great changes or even wars, but history is developing rapidly and smoothly, which is conducive to the generation of romanticism. Of course, romanticism and realism are closely linked. The idea that it is conducive to romanticism does not mean that it is harmful to realism, which has been repeatedly explained in my articles. Hereby I have to repeat it.

Lin Geng

Originally published in *Literature Review*, 1960 (12)

2 The High Tang Atmosphere

The High Tang marks the summit of classical Chinese poetry—an accolade not due to its quantity but due to its high quality. The number of poems in the High Tang is more than those in the Early Tang, but less than those in the Mid-Tang and Late Tang. *Complete Tang Poems* includes 2,757 poems by 270 Early Tang poets, 6,341 poems by 274 High Tang poets, 19,020 poems by 578 Mid-Tang poets, and 14,744 poems by 441 Late Tang poets, besides those by the poets in the Five Dynasties period (707–960) and a few anonymous non-prolific poets. If we plot a graph according to these figures, the Mid-Tang is obviously on the peak in the number of poets and poems, but we say that the High Tang is the summit of the Tang poetry, precisely for its quality.

The High Tang lasts about half a century, while the Early Tang covers about one century. Compared with the Early Tang, the High Tang made monumental progress in poetry writing. But in the Mid-Tang, its development slowed because of the difficulty in balancing profundity and simplicity, although the number of poems has increased, even as it made new achievements in some aspects. Then, in the Late Tang, it naturally became much less prolific. If the speed of development can reflect its essence, then the development of the High Tang poetry is its most vigorous and thriving moment.

I The High Tang Atmosphere is a reflection of the era

The High Tang Atmosphere refers to the burgeoning atmosphere in poetry, which is not only due to its grand development, but more importantly due to the characteristic burgeoning ideas and feelings which cannot be separated from that era. The High Tang Atmosphere is, therefore, a reflection of the spirit of the High Tang. However, if we think that poetry is like a camera, completely and slavishly reflecting the spiritual outlook of the time, it is not totally reasonable, because literature often reflects surrounding reality through the author's ideas and feelings. Especially in classical lyric poetry, the author's world view is often unified with the artistic image of his work. Of course, this does not mean that there are no subjective and objective contradictions in classical lyric poetry. For example, in a famous poem "Looking at the Wild" by Wang Ji in the Early Tang:

> At the East Highland, I look in the twilight.
> Where should I be after much travelling?
> Each tree is enveloped in autumn light;
> Each hill stands still in the sunset glowing.
> Shepherd boys are taking their calves back home,
> On the back of hunting steeds, birds perching.
> Looking around, I can find no friend close.
> Missing hermits, "Picking Vetches" I sing.

As a remnant of the late Sui Dynasty, the writer has a lonely feeling about the new unification in the Tang Dynasty. The lonely feeling of the remnants is expressed with the theme of this poem as in "At the East Highland, I look in the twilight. / Where should I be after much travelling?... Looking around, I can find no friend close. / Missing hermits, 'Picking Vetches' I sing". The reason this poem becomes a famous work in the Early Tang is not owing to this theme, but due to the striking images in the four middle lines: "Each tree is enveloped in autumn light; / Each hill stands still in the sunset glowing. / Shepherd boys are taking their calves back home, / On the back of hunting steeds, birds perching". These images, earlier than all other poems in the Early Tang, reflect people's comfortable feelings in the peaceful living environment of the newly unified kingdom. That is why this poem is so highly acclaimed in literary history. Even though this kind of praise of the time is not consistent with the remnants' world views, it is an objective reality reflected beyond the author's world view.

However, in classical lyric poetry, such phenomena are generally scarce, or at least unapparent. Generally speaking, the spirit of the era is often determined by the author's world views and personality nurtured in it. Thus, inevitably, the spirit of the era is reflected in poetry a little later than the development of the reality of that era. Because the understanding of the reality often lags behind its development, it often takes a short time for poets to fully understand the new reality, and to adapt the world views and personality they have developed at the previous stage. It's impossible for poets to closely follow the reality step by step. In fact, at the beginning of the Kaiyuan era, the whole society began to flourish after the development of Wu Zetian's imperial court. However, the summit of the poetry circle has to wait until the middle of the Kaiyuan era. In *Anthology of Poems: Spirit of Mountains and Rivers* we find:

> At the end of the Zhenguan era (c. 650), the artistic standard gradually rose; in the middle of the Jingyun era (710), it became quite far-sighted; after the 15th year of the Kaiyuan era (727), the rhythmic theory and spirit began to mature.

22 The High Tang Atmosphere

The middle of Jingyun (710) is actually the eve of Kaiyuan (713), but why did "the rhythmic theory and spirit not begin to mature" only until the 15th year of Kaiyuan? It's because the development and maturity of a kind of "atmosphere" or "style" cannot be achieved in one day. It can be seen in Cao Zhi, a representative of the Jian'an era when we look far back. Most of his famous works were in the late period of Jian'an, and some were written even after the Jian'an era. Moreover, numerous frontier fortress poems by Cen Shen considered as one of the achievements of the High Tang poetry were written shortly before the An Shi Rebellion. The influence of an era will not appear all of a sudden, nor will it disappear abruptly. Especially in the thousands of years of feudal society, its development is slow; it is natural that people need eight to ten years or even a longer time to understand it fully. The significance of the An Shi Rebellion, which is the watershed of the peak of the Tang Dynasty and the development of the feudal society for thousands of years, was seldom noticed by the people at that time. Except for Li Bai and Du Fu, other poets hardly reflected on this important event.

Especially because the An Shi Rebellion occurred only two years before the recovery of the capital Chang'an, it is easier for people at that time to think that it is just a temporary misfortune. Thus, even if the dark side of society has shown signs before the An Shi Rebellion, it is still difficult to immediately change the general feelings of life nurtured in the Prosperity of Kaiyuan for a long time. The contradictions and struggles between the dark and the bright side are inevitable in any era. In the High Tang, the confrontations between the two are also changing gradually. Generally speaking, regarding the spiritual outlook of the society before the Yunnan War in the tenth year (751) of Tianbao (742–756), the bright side is still predominant. Thus, Li Bai's "Ancient Style" No. 1 states:

> The white sun on the Purple Palace,
> Three ministers balance their power.
> The world unified as a whole,
> The Four Seas are peaceful and fair.

This is Li Bai's description of the society before the Yunnan War. At that time, Prime Minister Li Linfu (683–753) was indeed a destroyer of the enlightened politics by fawning on powerful dignitaries and killing virtuous and able people. But Li Linfu had a clear estimation of himself and dared not act very badly under the pressure of the enlightened political tradition. Historical records show that he eliminated his dissidents to maintain his own position, but tried to act in accordance with the rules on various policies, stabilizing the whole society until the tenth year of Tianbao. However, Yang Guozhong (?–756) was ambitious and craved for success recklessly. In this way, the situation became severe when the Yangs monopolised power in the 11th year of Tianbao and famine continued in the following two years. After the An Shi Rebellion, the Tang Empire sustained for about one and a half centuries, indicating that after this epoch-making turning point, it began to go downhill, but it did not immediately collapse. Moreover, before the An Shi Rebellion, as Li Bai writes in the "Ancient Style" No. 46:

> In one hundred and forty years,
> How impressive is the nation!

Although there are contradictions and turns, they are unified in a spectacular development, which forms the basis of the High Tang Atmosphere.

II The High Tang Atmosphere and Chen Zi'ang

The High Tang Atmosphere reflects the spirit of the era. However, it is obviously wrong to think that the High Tang Atmosphere is the flattery of the feudal ruling class, which is the main content of the poems written upon the emperor's orders, though never representing the High Tang Atmosphere. The High Tang Atmosphere praises the victory of the people, without which there is no High Tang Atmosphere. The prosperity of the Tang Dynasty is due to not only the peasant uprisings at the end of the Sui Dynasty, which forced the ruling class to make concessions, but the growing demand for democracy on those concessions since the Jian'an era. Thus, the feudal society developed smoothly at its rising stage. These are the fruits of people's struggles. The High Tang is not a gift from the ruling class. Therefore, the praise of the era is totally different from the so-called flattery. On the contrary, to praise the High Tang is to praise the spiritual force that promotes the liberation of society, and people's abundant real-life feelings and pride in victory. As the pioneer of the High Tang poetry circle, Chen Zi'ang is also a bridge between the High Tang Atmosphere and the Jian'an Spirit. Moreover, he is not satisfied with his status quo. His most famous "Song of Mounting the Youzhou Terrace" reads thus:

> Before, no ancients were seen;
> After, no followers will be seen.
> How vast the sky and earth are;
> Alone, I feel sad and shed tears.

This soul-stirring poem inspires people's entrepreneurial spirit and enhances their heroic temperament for breaking through the status quo. As a passion for ideals, and a fresh quality of positive romanticism, it is the most profound and indelible impression Chen Zi'ang made on the history of poetry. But if we think Chen Zi'ang is mainly exposing the darkness, or reflecting on a hopeless and declining era, would not it twist the historical truth? In fact, what Chen Zi'ang unveils here is the prelude to the High Tang. It shows that a poem reflecting on a rising era is not always singing the praises of peaceful development, let alone offering flattery. Chen Zi'ang

24 *The High Tang Atmosphere*

and Li Bai are two brilliant stars similar in their poetic viewpoints. Chen Zi'ang's poems such as the "Song of Mounting the Youzhou Terrace" are extremely similar to those by Li Bai such as "The Roads are Hard". If the eras that Chen Zi'ang and Li Bai have reflections on are declining, then what is the historic summit in the rise of the Tang Dynasty? If one of them reflects on the rising times while the other on the declining times, how can we understand their numerous similarities from poetic viewpoints to poetic writings? In fact, Chen Zi'ang foretells the High Tang, which Li Bai is singing highly of; they bear a high resemblance to each other. Moreover, it's the historic summit during the rising development lasting for one and a half centuries that gives birth to such poets. The mistakes of interpreting the High Tang Atmosphere as flattery or the simplified understanding of liberating poems as reflections on the intensified contradictions inevitably lead to confusions in understanding.

Contradictions are indispensable in social development. Is it rational that we cannot bear to see any contradiction in the poems reflecting the rising development at that time? Without understanding this point, it would almost be impossible to understand why it is on the eve of the High Tang that Chen Zi'ang wrote the "Song of Mounting the Youzhou Terrace" that aroused the attention of the whole era.

III The High Tang Atmosphere and the Jian'an Spirit

In reflecting on the ideal era in the history of Chinese poetry, most people think it is Jian'an that they longed for before the Tang Dynasty, and the High Tang afterwards. The High Tang Atmosphere, a step forward in the development of the Jian'an Spirit, makes the High Tang an unforgettable era. The earliest vigorous advocacy of the Jian'an Spirit is found in *Poetry Appreciation* by Zhong Rong, an outstanding critic in the Liang Dynasty (502–557). Afterwards, Chen Zi'ang's preface to "On Long Bamboos" argues,

> The Han and Wei Spirit is not passed down to the Jin and Song of the Southern Dynasties.

Such a powerful opinion pointed out the clear direction for the Tang poetry. After that, Li Bai writes in "Ancient Style" No. 1:

> Starting from the Jian'an era,
> People cherish not the flowery.

In "Farewell to My Uncle Collator Yun at Pavilion Xie Tiao in Xuancheng", we read:

> Your Penglai writing has the Jian'an bone
> And in the middle a touch of Xie's freshness.

All of us have vigorous thought without end,
Almost near the sky to touch the bright moon.

A special collection of the poems written in the High Tang, *Anthology of Poems: Spirit of Mountains and Rivers* by Yin Fan, states:

> After the 15th year of the Kaiyuan era, the rhythmic theory and spirit began to mature. It inherited the spirit from Jian'an; as for the musicality, even the Taikang period (280–289) in the Western Jin Dynasty (266–316) is not comparable.

It can be seen that the spirit is one of the characteristics of the Jian'an poetry as well as the fine tradition of the Tang poetry. Thus, he says in reference to Gao Shi: "Gao Shi's poems are mostly out of his heart, and spirited at the same time". On Cui Hao, he says: "When he grew old, he changed his style to be normal, with an awe-inspiring spirit".

However, it is an indisputable historical fact that the High Tang Atmosphere inherited the Jian'an Spirit. So, what are the similarities between the High Tang and the Jian'an era? What are the differences between the High Tang Atmosphere and the Jian'an Spirit? To answer these questions, we must first understand that the Jian'an era was an era of liberation from the imperial power of the Two Han Dynasties and from the yoke of dull feudal ethics, and that Jian'an literature was effectively liberated from aristocratic literature for people's victorious feelings and democratic demands. The free-running romantic temperament and the bright image of optimism constituted the spiritual essence of the Jian'an Spirit. The Tang Dynasty was also liberated from the powerful families in the Six Dynasties, from the nihilistic tendencies of Buddhism, and from weak partial sovereignty and long-term division. Thus, its literariness was liberated from the luxurious tendencies with a higher sense of victory, more mature democratic beliefs, more heroic romantic temperament, and more abundant and open-hearted singing, and appeared in the history of poetry. The remaining powerful families in society and the remnant poetic influence of the Qi and Liang Dynasties in the Early Tang were swept away for the High Tang. The power of liberation is the truly excellent tradition of the Jian'an Spirit. Did such a developing force have no conflict with the backward and conservative forces in society? It was like gorgeous waves bursting on the rocks of conflicts and reflected as a complex singing. On the whole, it was unified as the people's victorious voice, "the High Tang Voice" that people avidly sought. The magnificent power of the Tang Dynasty was manifested in economy, culture, frontier defence as well as in the universal daily lives. If these forces are not the strength of the people, whose strength is it? And if it is not the people who have emancipated these forces, then who does? This is the essence of the burgeoning High Tang Atmosphere. However, a few scholars think that the High Tang Atmosphere must be flattery. It seems that they failed to

26   *The High Tang Atmosphere*

see the power of the people in the High Tang, or they think the people in the High Tang were powerless so that they could only flatter the ruling power. This is the key issue in many arguments about the High Tang Atmosphere.

Jian'an is not only a liberated era but a difficult era. It is difficult because it appeared amid the war-torn ruins, and because there still lacked an effective experience to help the liberation as everything seemed to be casually made. A kind of desolate and high-pitched singing is the keynote of the Jian'an Spirit, as shown in "A sudden wind blows over the white sun" and "A high terrace has more sad wind". The High Tang appeared in a time of ever-rising development of peace and prosperity over a century. Equipped with the mature ways of democratic struggle in the feudal society through hundreds of years, it is a liberating era that underwent relatively smooth progress. Both the High Tang Atmosphere and the Jian'an Spirit are liberating, but not totally the same, because the former has a kind of self-confident and delightful prospect, as shown in such lines as "Heaven-made talents, we weren't made in vain", "The Yellow River falls from the Heaven", "The road is as bright as the sky", and "The bright moon rising at Mt. Heaven". Of course, to ensure and achieve this peak of liberation, people have to struggle with the constant spirit of withstanding hardships. Therefore, the Jian'an Spirit is not only in the midst of the High Tang Atmosphere, but its backbone. Without this backbone, the High Tang Atmosphere would have been impossible. That is why Chen Zi'ang's strong advocate of the spirit has such a great significance in the history of poetry, and why Li Bai praises "the Jian'an Bone". However, the High Tang Atmosphere is more than the "bone". It also has strong muscles strongly supporting the "bone". The Jian'an Spirit is shown in Liu Zhen's poem "To My Younger Brother":

> Graceful are pines on the mountain;
> Wild is the wind in the valley.
> How strong the sound of the wind is!
> How powerful pine branches are!
> The ice-frost is miserable,
> But the pines are always upright.
> Not suffering from the freezing cold?
> Pine and cypress have their own nature.

This is what is praised as "the real bone endures the frost; the high wind is beyond conventions" in *Poetry Appreciation*. If so, the High Tang Atmosphere is the singing of the Spring as in "The sunny spring fascinates me with misty scenes; / Nature provides me food of thought on my writing". They are essentially the same. However, the High Tang Atmosphere further shows that this essence plays a more important role in life. Imperceptible and ubiquitous, it is better described as an atmosphere, rather than a simple and plain spirit. It is a more abundant development of the Jian'an Spirit.

The High Tang Atmosphere, just like the Jian'an Spirit, is a traditional poetic concept. It reflects the characteristics of the High Tang, but it is not always understood directly as the spiritual outlook of the era, although it does reflect on it. It has an obviously different keynote from the poetry of the time when people's power was constrained and taken down, which is the so-called time of apparent contradictions when people have difficulty in making their living and finding a way out in the long feudal society. The keynotes reflected in poetry are gloomy as if all the colours had lost their brilliance in the grey atmosphere. Similar to those of the Jian'an Spirit, the keynotes are hearty, and colours are bright in the High Tang Atmosphere. They are heartier and brighter even than those of Jian'an. That is the relationship between the High Tang Atmosphere and the Jian'an Spirit.

IV The High Tang Atmosphere is an artistic image with the characteristics of the era

What is called the "High Tang Atmosphere"? Or first, what is the atmosphere? *Poetry Styles* by Jiao Ran of the Tang says:

The intense atmosphere is due to the deep understanding of the potential.

In "Clarifying the Potential", it also says:

The writings by creative masters are like climbing the Jingshan Mountain and Wushan Mountain to see the three tributaries of the Xiang River and scenic spots of the states of Yan and Ying. It has thousands of roundabouts, changes and forms. Each mountain soaring into the sky above stands alone with a great atmosphere and soaring potential but harmoniously, while the long river shines with no waves for ten thousand *li*, showing a highly complex and circuitous shape. Outstanding styles past and present all have reached the peaks.

"Clarifying the Potential" is to make clear the possible. The so-called "great atmosphere and soaring potential" shows the close relationship between atmosphere and potential. The concepts of the High Tang Atmosphere are described in

The writings by creative masters are like climbing the Jingshan Mountain and Wushan Mountain to see the three tributaries of the Xiang River and scenic spots of the states of Yan and Ying. It has thousands of roundabouts, changes and forms.

The concept of "intense atmosphere" is formed on the basis of the High Tang poetry and elaborated by the contemporary Jiao Ran and Yin Fan,

28 *The High Tang Atmosphere*

and later generations yearn for the High Tang mainly because of this atmosphere. Jiang Kui says in *Taoist White Stone's Poetic Comments*:

> The atmosphere should be dense, but it may fail and become crude; the potency should be immense, but it may fail and become insane.

The "potency" here is similar to the "potential" in *Poetry Styles*. The above-mentioned "it may fail and become insane" well explains that the "immense" is with "great atmosphere and soaring potential"; thus, it "may fail", and becomes "insane". And "The atmosphere should be dense" mentioned above is similar to "the intense atmosphere" in *Poetry Styles*. Because the atmosphere is "dense" and "intense", it seems shallow and crude, but is actually profound and soaring. *Azure Stream Poetic Remarks* notes: "Writers in the High Tang may seem coarse but not coarse, clumsy but not clumsy". If they are really coarse and clumsy, they are crude; this is the accomplishment of "profundity out of simplicity" in the High Tang poetry, making two to three words equal to endless statements, which is considered "intense" or "dense". Therefore, the preface of *Poetry Styles* says:

> Authentic and outstanding sentences compete with Nature, which can be understood but hard to express.

Taoist White Stone's Poetic Comments quotes Su Dongpo as saying:

> Limited words have endless senses, which are the best words in the world.

They all emphasise that the highest attainment of poetry is to be sensorially rich until it is inexpressible, and to be complete until it is authentic and natural. And today we should further understand that to achieve such attainments, of course, requires the poet's artistry, but more importantly the rich and profound living content of poetry, without which the artistry cannot be improved. However, the "dense" or "intense" atmosphere prevailing in the High Tang poems proves that it is a reflection of the whole era's spirit, not belonging to a single poet.

Therefore, the essence of "the High Tang Atmosphere" and "the High Tang Voice" is the burgeoning vitality and the youthful melody. In *Poetic Remarks in the Quite Ideal Residence* by Zhu Yizun (1629–1709), there is such a quote:

> The Tang poems are fresh and bright as if they were just born out of writing brushes and inkstones the other day. But contemporary poems are already old-fashioned the moment they are created.

This creative and liberated era gave birth to distinct characters, and liberated the poets' personality so that those poems are always vibrant, as fresh as they are just born out of writing brushes and inkstones the other day, and so rich that they can only be illustrated with an atmosphere. Of course, the "atmosphere" is a more abstract concept, not as specific as "spirit". However, as an ideal artistic image in ancient poetry, the "High Tang Atmosphere" is as concrete as the "Jian'an Spirit". The use of a more abstract concept than the spirit is due to its more abundant connotation, and when this abstract concept is specifically explained, it has a typical universal significance. This is why the "High Tang Atmosphere" is avidly sought in general by ancient poets after the "Jian'an Spirit".

V On the High Tang Atmosphere in *Azure Stream Poetic Remarks*

The most concentrated work on the "High Tang Atmosphere" is Yan Yu's *Azure Stream Poetic Remarks*. The central proposition of this critical masterpiece is to advocate the "High Tang Atmosphere". Its opinions, in fact, inherited the traditional understanding of the "Jian'an Spirit" and the "High Tang Atmosphere", integrated the opinions from *Poetry Appreciation* to *Poetry Styles*, and finally reached a conclusion:

> Tracing back to the Han and Wei Dynasties, I still resolutely believe that the High Tang determines the rules of poetry. Even though I would be criticised in the world, I still insist on that.

He says:

> Remarks on poetry are similar to those on the Buddhist meditation; thus, the Han, Wei, and Jin poetries and the High Tang poetry are the first ranks.

The so-called Han, Wei, and Jin poetries refer to those with the Jian'an Spirit. He says,

> After the Huangchu period (220–226), only Ruan Ji's 'Poems on Feelings' are extremely elegant and antique with the Jian'an Spirit.

He also says:

> Besides Tao Yuanming (also Tao Qian, c. 365–427) and Ruan Sizong, only Zuo Taichong (also Zuo Si) is more talented than his contemporaries in the Jin Dynasty.

On Tao Yuanming, Zhong Rong's *Poetry Appreciation* states that he "also has Zuo Si's strength" (Zhong Rong believes that the "Jian'an Strength" and the "Jian'an Spirit" are actually the same). The reason why *Azure Stream*

30 *The High Tang Atmosphere*

Poetic Remarks added the Jin Dynasty to the traditional concept of the "Han and Wei Spirit" is that Ruan Ji, Zuo Si, and Tao Yuanming all have the Jian'an Spirit. This fine tradition became more ideal and rich in the High Tang, so people say that "As for the poems of the High Tang poets, none cannot be appreciated", and that "Tracing back to the Han and Wei Dynasties, I still resolutely believe that the High Tang determines the rules of poetry".

Azure Stream Poetic Remarks observes: "There are five rules in poetry: style, strength, atmosphere, interest, and musicality". Separately, there are five rules here. However, they can be combined into the atmosphere. For example,

> *West Clarity Poetic Remarks* recorded that in the collection of Tao Yuanming's poems in the residence of Chao Wenyuan, there was a poem "Asking the Messenger": "You came from the mountain / Heaven Eyes through night and day. / By my south window, how many / Chrysanthemums grow now? / Rose leaves wither away; / Autumn orchid smells sweet. / When you are back again, / The mountain wine is mellow. I believe that this poem is really good." However, its style and atmosphere are different from those of Yuanming. Isn't it a lost poem by Li Bai, but carelessly collected in Tao's collection by later generations?

The notion of "style and atmosphere" is similar to "The intense atmosphere is due to the deep understanding of the potential" in *Poetry Styles*. The two statements are closely related. The poetic styles discussed in *Azure Stream Poetic Remarks* include the Jian'an Style, the Classical Style, the High Tang Style, the Late Tang Style, the Shaoling Style, and the Taibai Style. Then, the so-called "style" is the characteristics of the era or the writers. As for "musicality", *Azure Stream Poetic Remarks* says:

> Words are best with rhythm, and writings are best with musicality. Reciting Meng Haoran's poems for long, people will hear the musical sound of metal and stone.

Then, the "musicality" is similar to "After the 15th year of the Kaiyuan era, the rhythmic theory and spirit began to mature" in *Anthology of Poems: Spirit of Mountains and Rivers*. It is not merely about the poetic patterns of the four tones, alliteration, and assonance. In *Anthology of Poems: Spirit of Mountains and Rivers* the belief is expressed that those who purposely pursue musicality are "advocating heresy and writing far-fetched lines", and that "although their knowledge can fill up bamboo suitcases, it's of no use!" whereas *Taoist White Stone's Poetic Comments* argues, "The words of a school have their own flavours, similar to the fact that each of the 24 tunes of music has its own musical sound". The tradition of relating the "flavour", or "style" to the "sound" and "tone" probably originated from *Classical Arguments: On Writing*. Then, the "musicality" in *Azure Stream Poetic Remarks* is also related to the style. We may say that among the five items listed in *Azure Stream Poetic Remarks*, "style" and "musicality" are relatively external, while "strength", "atmosphere", and "interest" are central concepts. The "Yezhong Collection" in *Poetry Styles* has a statement about Cao Zhi and Liu Zhen, two representatives of the Jian'an Spirit,

> Words ride with feelings; the situation arouses emotions. If not by intention, the atmosphere is high.

The "feelings" and "emotions" here are the "interest" in *Azure Stream Poetic Remarks*, and the "atmosphere" here is the "strength" in the same book. They are essentially the same as the "spirit" and the "atmosphere". Therefore, *Azure Stream Poetic Remarks* concludes:

> Poetry is the chanting of emotions and temperament. The High Tang poets only focus on interests.

To generalise the poet's stylistic accomplishments, the "atmosphere" is used in *Azure Stream Poetic Remarks*, for example:

> In the Tang Dynasty and the current Song Dynasty, poems are different in atmosphere, regardless of their skills.

Or,

> Before the Dali period (766–779), it is clearly a kind of language. In the Late Tang, it is clearly another kind of language. In the current dynasty, it is still another kind of language.

Or,

> 'At dawn, I ride a lame donkey in the east wind', a line in a quatrain, never shows the High Tang Atmosphere.

What is more prominent here is that *Azure Stream Poetic Remarks* uses "atmosphere" not only to assess the poetry of the High Tang, but to assess the poems in the Han, Wei, Jian'an or other times, so "atmosphere" is the most general concept. For example:

> Ancient poems in the Han and Wei Dynasties have a chaotic atmosphere where excellent lines are difficult to find.

32 *The High Tang Atmosphere*

Another example:

> Works in Jian'an are excellent in the atmosphere, impossible to find specific lines or words. Although Xie Kangle (also Xie Lingyun) imitated the poems by the Yezhong poets, his writings have a different atmosphere.

However, the Jian'an Spirit is also a kind of atmosphere. "Answers to Adopted Uncle Wu Jingxian in Lin'an" in *Azure Stream Poetic Remarks* declares:

> The poems of the High Tang poets, similar to the writing of Yan Lugong (also Yan Zhenqing), are both vigorous in strength and dense in atmosphere.

However, the highest standard of atmosphere is to be dense, which is also what *Poetry Styles* and *Taoist White Stone's Poetic Comments* insist. *Poetry Styles* rules:

> The atmosphere should be thick but not distended.

Taoist White Stone's Poetic Comments finds:

> The potency should be immense, but it may fail and become insane. The blood should run through smoothly, but it may fail and become a runoff.

"Answers to Adopted Uncle Wu Jingxian in Lin'an" has a commentary on the High Tang poetry:

> For poetry, the word "strong" is not suitable. It's not so appropriate as "potent" or "awe-inspiring" in *The Differentiation of Poetry* to describe the manners of poetry. Such nuances should also be differentiated. The poems by Su Dongpo and Huang Shangu are like the calligraphy of Mi Yuanzhang (also Mi Fu), vigorous in writing but finally with the forcible atmosphere of when Zilu served Confucius… With just this word, I find that my uncle's heels are not on the ground.

"Potent" and "awe-inspiring" are two of the "nine qualities poetry has" in *Azure Stream Poetic Remarks*. The "quality", or the style, "describes the manners of poetry", showing that the manner refers to the style at the same time, while the centre of style is attributed to the atmosphere, whose standard is to be dense. The High Tang Atmosphere is the highest ideal of atmospheres, so the word "strong" is not suitable, because it has the tendency of "distended", "insane", and "runoff", hence "finally with the forcible atmosphere of when Zilu served Confucius". The first of the *Twenty-Four Poems on Poetry Appreciation* by Sikong Tu of Tang is "Potent" saying that:

> Change the 'weak' into the 'dense', and accumulate the 'strong' to be 'potent'; thus, related to all things and unparalleled in space.

The ancients thought that the "strong" should be accumulated to be "potent", then the concept of "strong" is still not dense enough, and the reason why the "High Tang Atmosphere" is "dense" and "potent" is precisely that it is "related to all things and unparalleled in space", which is the essence of the "High Tang Atmosphere".

Azure Stream Poetic Remarks issues this judgement: "Ancient poems in the Han and Wei Dynasties have a chaotic atmosphere where excellent lines are difficult to find", then what is its difference from the "dense" characteristic of the "High Tang Atmosphere"? This is to be understood from another poetic point of view, that is, the remarks on "enlightenment" in *Azure Stream Poetic Remarks*. "Enlightenment", originally from Buddhist meditation, includes "gradual enlightenment" and "sudden enlightenment". *Azure Stream Poetic Remarks* is actually using "sudden enlightenment" to discuss poetry, as in:

> It is called 'straight to the origin', 'sudden enlightenment', and 'right to the point'.

Azure Stream Poetic Remarks borrowed the word "enlightenment" to discuss poetry, but Wu Jingxian expressed his opposition; thus, in "Answers to Adopted Uncle Wu Jingxian in Lin'an" we read,

> My uncle said that the discussion of Buddhist meditation is not in the language of scholars and Confucians. If we intend to make a poem understandable, but at first we have no intention to use the literary language, it would be out of question to employ the language of scholars and Confucians.

Then, what on earth is the "enlightenment" in *Azure Stream Poetic Remarks*? In fact, it's about capturing images. In a poem by Han Yu: "I am willing to have two wings / And chase in the eight directions. / In faith I'm suddenly enlightened: / A hundred strangeness in my guts". Poets fly in the vast space on the wings of rich imagination and chase the images he wants to create. This is exactly what is called "The writing is made by nature, / And the masters get it by chance". Therefore, *Azure Stream Poetic Remarks* opines:

> Moreover, Meng Xiangyang (also Meng Haoran) is much inferior to Han Tuizhi (also Han Yu) in academic ability, but his poems are much superior than Han's. That's because of simply the subtle enlightenment.

34   *The High Tang Atmosphere*

"Enlightenment" is "to chase"; "subtle enlightenment" is "to get it by chance". And images arouse the most direct feelings, which are "straight to the origin", and "right to the point". This opinion is also based on *Poetry Appreciation* by Zhong Rong. To quote from *Poetry Appreciation*:

> As for the singing of feelings and sentiments, what is more valuable than the use of natural phenomena and social activities? "Missing you like the flowing water" uses what is seen; "A high terrace has more sad winds" uses what people feel; "In early morning, I mount the Longshan mountain" has no allusion, and "The bright moon is shining on the snow" is not from classics or history. Most of the best expressions, ancient or modern, are not supplementary allusions, but directly created.

The expression "directly created" in *Poetry Appreciation* is to seize such impressive and direct images as in "A high terrace has more sad winds" and "The bright moon is shining on the snow". Similar to *Poetry Appreciation*, *Azure Stream Poetic Remarks* also has a large paragraph on the same idea:

> Poets sing of feelings and sentiments. The High Tang poets... have endless senses with limited words. Writers in modern times propose unusual interpretations of their words. Then they write poems on words, or on talents, or on discussions. Though refined, their poems are different from the ancients', probably because they lack the style of "one singing and three sighs". And they prefer phenomena or activities to interest in their works. Every word and every rhyme they use have sources. However, after reading several times, I still have no idea about their purposes.

The expressions such as "no allusion", "not from classics or history", and "directly created" in *Poetry Appreciation* are similar to "simply the subtle enlightenment", "straight to the origin", and "right to the point" in *Azure Stream Poetic Remarks*. The "supplementary allusions" opposed in *Poetry Appreciation* is also similar to "poems on words" and "poems on talents" opposed in *Azure Stream Poetic Remarks*. "Poems on discussion" are also seen in the author's words:

> Poems have special styles, but they are not about books. Poems have special interests, but they are not about reasons. However, if we don't read enough books, or understand more reasons thoroughly, we are not able to reach the peak of writing. The best poets are not determined by reasoning, or constrained by words.

I have to emphasise that he thinks that poets who pursue a high degree of artistic achievement need to read more books and understand more reasons. However, when they write poems, they are "not determined by reasoning, or constrained by words". It is precisely because the poem aims to seize the most direct images, which should naturally contain the "books" read, and the "reasons" understood. Therefore, "the Tang people sing highly of disposition, while reasons are in it". Furthermore, in the Han and Wei Dynasties this "disposition" is described as follows:

> In the Han and Wei poetry, reasons and disposition have left no trace. Ancient poems in the Han and Wei Dynasties have a chaotic atmosphere where excellent lines are difficult to find.

We further prove it with another passage in *Azure Stream Poetic Remarks*:

> Only enlightenment is the right way and the natural way. However, there are deep and shallow enlightenment of different types. There is thorough enlightenment and half enlightenment. The Han and Wei poems are superior, not relying on enlightenment... The High Tang poets have thorough enlightenment. Though others have enlightenment, they are not in the first rank.
>
> The High Tang poets only focus on their interests, like a sleeping magical antelope hanging itself with its horns, leaving no trace on the ground. Thus its brilliance is thorough and exquisite, not pieced together.

To sum up, the Han and Wei poetry has "a chaotic atmosphere" "not relying on enlightenment", and "reasons and disposition" "leaving no trace". The High Tang is characterised by a "dense atmosphere", and "thorough enlightenment", "singing highly of disposition, while reasons are in it", and it "only focuses on interests ... exquisite and thorough". If "enlightenment" is the pursuit of images, then the Han and Wei poets did not pursue them intentionally, but waited for them naturally, so that they are "not relying on enlightenment"; the High Tang poets realised the significance of pursuit and reached the attainments of profundity in simplicity, so they have "a thorough enlightenment". Since the Han and Wei poets did not strive to capture images, the images were simple but complete; thus, "excellent lines are difficult to find"; it's like an unexplored mine, or "a chaotic atmosphere". The High Tang poets, however, endeavoured to capture and obtain the most direct and distinct images. It seems as if the mine of real gold and jade has been explored and is shining with beautiful and extraordinary brilliance, which cannot be chaotic, but is in a dense atmosphere. However, in *Azure Stream Poetic Remarks*, the term "enlightenment" is the capture of images, the "disposition" or "interest" is the triumph of imagination, the "thoroughness" means to directly seek profundity out of simplicity, and the "atmosphere" is about the style and manner. The word "dense" is used to show the vitality and fullness of the style and manner, which is the reflection of the High Tang Spirit.

36 *The High Tang Atmosphere*

VI The artistic characteristics of the High Tang Atmosphere

By virtue of the poets' rich imagination of life and combined with the mature development of poetry in ideas and arts since Jian'an, the High Tang Atmosphere is flying in the vast and burgeoning open space and describing the distinct characteristics of that era. Then the artistic features of this image cannot exist independent of that time. Therefore, its artistic characters are inseparable from the characteristics of the era.

The most prominent feature of the High Tang Atmosphere is the vigour and vitality, fresh and bright as if they were just born out of writing brushes and inkstones the other day, which is also one of the hallmarks of the High Tang. The High Tang produced artistic images full of ideas and feelings, showing a high degree of unity of ideological and artistic quality. It is biased if we believe that only the revelation of darkness is an ideological work. We can only say that the works belonging to the people are ideological works, and that the people do not always describe darkness. Taking as an example the folk songs, an important source of art, the vast majority are singing of love. In "Airs of the States", folk songs such as "Huge Rats" condemning greedy officials are in the minority. People's desire for a happy life naturally forms a force against the dark side. How can there be no ideological content here? Its ideological content lies in that it belongs to the people. It is also illogical for some people to think that the positive romanticism in the Tang poetry is inevitably revealing the darkness because positive romanticists are not satisfied with the status quo. Discontent with the status quo, of course, can reveal the darkness, but it can also be the pursuit of ideals. Moreover, a general understanding of the spirit of positive romanticism, especially in classical Chinese poetry, often falls in the latter category. Needless to say, Qu Yuan's "Nine Songs" has no specific revelation of the dark side. Even in "Li Sao", the most representative work of Qu Yuan, there are just a few specific descriptions of the dark side, and our deepest impression is of his personality with a strong pursuit of ideals and brilliancy. Of course, the pursuit of brilliance and the dark side, the two sides of a contradiction, are antagonistic. But, whether the author sings to reveal more darkness or to praise more sunny subjects will result in different images, which are, in fact, reflecting the spirit of the era. When the power of light, in reality, is suppressed and the dark force runs rampant, exposing the darkness becomes the main writing approach; when the power of the bright side develops, and the dark force has to give in, the passionate pursuit of ideals becomes the most direct singing. Qu Yuan's era is an era of rapid development in the pre-Qin Dynasty, and also an era in which the economy, politics, and culture of ancient China leap forward most vigorously. The various colourful images in Qu Yuan's works are just a reflection of this era, which is consistent with his positive romantic spirit and romantic creative approaches. Similar to Qu Yuan, Li Bai appeared at the peak of the High Tang. A few poems in Li Bai's "Ancient Style" revealed the darkness, which is only one aspect of his poetry achievements. His main achievement and typical image in the history of poetry is his heroic *yuefu* ballads shown in such lines as "A hundred poems for a barrel of wine". The pursuit of ideals is the main aspect of his works. The reason why Li Bai is regarded as a poet with a positive romantic spirit is that he adopted a romantic writing approach, mainly reflected in such works rather than in his fewer "Ancient Style" poems. Li Bai is the most typical poet of the High Tang, and the High Tang Atmosphere is the singing of the positive themes favoured by the people, reflecting people's increasing power in this era. This is the characteristic of the High Tang Atmosphere; it belongs to the people and favoured by the people, and it is antagonistic to the dark power and conservative forces. This is its ideological content.

Different from the Warring States period (475–221 BCE) with so many breath-taking changes in life, the High Tang is a unified era, an era of peaceful life and prosperous development. Therefore, it is more plain and open-hearted in character. Compared with "Airs of the States", *Chuci* is much more complicated and tortuous, while the Tang poetry is closer in style. This style of profundity in simplicity and of burgeoning atmosphere is unique in the Tang poetry. Wang Wei's "Song of Youth" states:

> The New Home wine worth ten thousand is so mellow,
> Enticing young roaming swordsmen in Xianyang town.
> They drink heartily to their spirit and renown,
> Leaving their steeds by a high inn to weeping willows.

"Song of Yingzhou" by Gao Shi describes:

> The Yingzhou youngsters are happy with the wild plain,
> Hunting outside the city wall in fox fur robes fine.
> Not drunken with a thousand cups of Captive wine,
> The Hu nomads can ride steeds at the age of ten.

Li Bai's "Looking at the Sky-Gate Mount" depicts:

> The Sky-Gate Mount is split open by the Chu River.
> The blue water eastward begins to flow northward.
> Green mountains on both sides are facing each other.
> A lonely sail comes into sight from near the sun.

And his "Ballad of Mount Lu" sings:

> Mount Lu stands up to the South Dipper high above
> Like a gigantic nine-fold stone screen of brocade.
> Climbing to view the spectacular heaven and earth:
> The long river flows eastward and never returns;
> The yellow clouds of ten thousand li move in the wind;
> Nine white waves are running down from the snowy mount.

38 *The High Tang Atmosphere*

A youthful melody with a promising prospect is the general characteristic of the High Tang poetry. Li Bai's "Song of the Hengjiang River" reads:

> People say Hengjiang is good,
> But you say Hengjiang is evil.
> The river wind can blow down a hill in three days;
> Its white waves are higher than the Waguan tower.

Facing the dangerous surging waves, he wrote out such a spectacular scene, making it a grand song of the era, similar to the soul-stirring "Hard are the Trails of Shu". Is this short poem like a folk song saying "Hengjiang is evil" or is it deeply praising "Hengjiang is good"? This is a rich singing voice in real life. Contradictions are unavoidable in real life, but the overwhelming brilliant image shows the growth of an era's character that can withstand the surging waves. Thus, Li Bai's poetry is typical in the High Tang. In fact, the character of this era is universally present. Du Fu's "Out of the Frontier: Latter" says:

> At dawn, we entered the East Camp;
> At dusk we were on the Sunny Bridge.
> The setting sun shines on the flag.
> The wind blows, and the horses neigh.
> Ten thousand tents in the desert,
> Each officer convenes his men.
> The bright moon hanging in the sky,
> The curfew makes the night lonely.
> Army reeds make sad noises;
> Warriors, though proud, feel solemn.
> Can we know the general's name?
> Might be the Swift General Huo!

This is really a "vigorous and soul-stirring" poem. In classical Chinese poetry, it only belongs to the High Tang. In Wang Changling's "Song of Fortress" No. 2, we read:

> I water my horse and cross the river
> In autumn, water cold and wind sword-like.
> In the vast desert, the sun has not set,
> And Lintao is seen far away in dark.
> About the fierce battle of the Great Wall,
> All border guards talk with a high spirit.
> Since ancient till now, in the yellow dust
> Lots of white bones are cluttered with wild weeds.

Being dense, open-hearted, typical, and vivid, it is the most vigorous and powerful singing. In Li Bai's "Bringing in the Wine":

> The Yellow River falls from the Heaven,
> Rushing into the sea with no return!
> A strong five-dappled horse,
> A thousand-gold fir coat,
> I'll call my son to exchange for the wine mellow,
> And kill with you thousands of years of sorrow.

Literally, he already has "thousands of years of sorrow". Isn't the emotion heavy? However, it is precisely the "thousands of years of sorrow" that is dense enough to match the High Tang Atmosphere, to relate to and compete with the atmosphere in the "Song of Mounting the Youzhou Terrace": "Before, no ancients were seen; / After, no followers will be seen. / How vast the sky and earth are; / Alone, I feel sad and shed tears!" Additionally, it shows that the peak of the High Tang poetry is more magnificent than that of Chen Zi'ang. However, if we think that "white hair of ten thousand metres" and "kill with you thousands of years of sorrow" are only about the huge amount and endurance of sorrow, we are still at the literal level. A deeper understanding of the image should focus on its fullness and vividness, which is the real accomplishment of the High Tang Atmosphere. "Yu the Beauty" by the last emperor (Li Yu) of the Southern Tang Dynasty (937–976) features these verses:

> If you ask me how much sorrow I'm suffering,
> It is like the Yangtze River flowing eastward in spring.

The two famous lines are also vivid about the huge amount and endurance of sorrow. However, this image never belongs to the High Tang Atmosphere. The sorrow is indeed heavy and long, but it is expressed so pitifully. In terms of image, "It is like the Yangtze River flowing eastward in spring" and "The Yellow River falls from the Heaven" are simply incomparable with completely different personalities. Isn't the Yangtze River longer than the Yellow River? Is it obligatory to use the "Yangtze River" and "the Yellow River" to form the "High Tang Atmosphere"? Here follows Wang Changling's "Seeing off Xin Jian at the Lotus Tower":

> When cold rain came to River Wu at night,
> I bid farewell at Mount Chu alone at dawn.
> If my friends in Luoyang ask about me:
> A piece of ice heart is in a jade pot.

This is also a typical example of the High Tang Atmosphere. The High Tang Atmosphere is full and burgeoning because it is abundant in every corner

40   *The High Tang Atmosphere*

of life; it seems not exaggerating when it in fact uses exaggeration in "white hair of ten thousand metres". It seems not small in "A piece of ice heart is in a jade pot". Just like a small dandelion, it represents the whole spring world. It is exquisite and thorough, but still dense. It is sorrowful in a thousand ways but still open-hearted. Rooted in the great enthusiasm of life and the sensitivity about new things, it grows with the liberation of people's power in the developing times. It brings sunny, rich, and healthy aesthetic attainments. This is the High Tang Atmosphere belonging to the people and aspired to by the past dynasties.

The High Tang Atmosphere is the characteristic image of the era. It is the general keynote of the High Tang poetry. However, this does not prevent a few poems in the High Tang from being different from this atmosphere or keynote, nor does it prevent the occasional occurrence of this atmosphere in poems after the High Tang. For example, Liu Fangping lived in the High Tang, but his poem "Moonlit Night" states:

> In deep night, the moon only lights half of the house.
> The Big Dipper shows its shape; the South Dipper tilts.
> Tonight I get to know the coming of warm spring:
> Outside the green window screen, there are beetles chirping.

Another is "Spring Complaint":

> Outside window screens, the sun sets into the dusk.
> In the golden house, no one can see the sad tears.
> In the lonely and empty courtyard, spring would stay.
> Pear blossoms all over the ground, the door is shut.

It is like the atmosphere in the Mid-Tang and Late Tang. Lu Lun, a poet of the Dali period, wrote the "Song of Fortress":

> The wind shaking the grass in dark woods,
> The general shot his bow at night.
> At dawn back for the white arrow,
> He found it's stuck in the stone ridge.
> In the dim moonlight, geese flew high.
> At night the Tartar chief fled away.
> We'd chase him down with light riders,
> But thick snow fell on our bows and swords.

It still shows the High Tang Atmosphere. Therefore, *Azure Stream Poetic Remarks* says that the good poems in Dali still followed the High Tang, but the bad ones gradually became dispirited and fell into the Late Tang. It also says that "A few poems by the High Tang poets led the trend for the Late Tang, but a few by the Late Tang poets can be listed in the High Tang. It's just a generalisation of their styles". Regarding the character of an era, certainly it can only be a generalisation. Therefore, the High Tang Atmosphere represents all the achievements of a poetic era, and countless outstanding poets have contributed to the thriving atmosphere. It is also the ideal of classical Chinese poetry because it is distinct, open-hearted, simple but profound; the vivid images, rich imagination, and abundant feelings are united into rich and endless expressions with ideological and artistic achievements. This is also known as the "dense" style of the High Tang Atmosphere.

In history, nobody knows how many poets are looking forward to this High Tang Atmosphere, but it is a product and reflection of the era; after the High Tang, China has been trapped in the mud of the declining feudal society for a long time from the Song (960–1279), Yuan (1271–1368), Ming (1368–1644), and Qing (1636–1912) Dynasties. This splendid peak of poetic achievements has become a promising but inaccessible admiration in classical Chinese poetry for over a thousand years.

Conclusion

Today, the High Tang Atmosphere as we have discussed is understood as a phenomenon in the history of Chinese poetry and accepted as an abundant treasure in the literary heritage. Today, we are happily entering a more heroic era that entirely belongs to the people. When we look back at such a glorious era in the history of Chinese poetry, we are smiling; let the outstanding achievements of classical Chinese poetry enrich our creation today and inspire us to shape a more brilliant characteristic image in the era of our own.

27 January 1958

Originally published in the *Journal of Peking University*, 1958 (2)

3 Symbols at the peak of the Tang poetry

The Tang poetry marks the peak in the development of classical Chinese poetry, which is due to the maturity of ancient Chinese feudal society in political, economic, cultural, and other aspects as well as the long-term development and final maturity of ancient Chinese poetry represented by the five- and seven-character poetry. The two processes of maturity are long and tortuous. After the unification of the Sui and Tang Dynasties, both of them reached the peak step by step. More powerful than only one peak, the confluence of the two peaks made the Tang poetry burgeoning and magnificent. It left us an unforgettable impression like the refreshing spring breeze, and thousands of miles of blue sky.

From the perspective of social development, the unification of the Sui and Tang Dynasties is similar to that of the Qin and Han Dynasties. Before the latter, over 400 years of the Spring and Autumn and Warring States periods (770–221 BCE) witnessed a historical process from division to unification through many wars and battles; so did the nearly 400 years of the Wei, Jin, and Six Dynasties before the unification of the Sui and Tang Dynasties. The unified Qin Dynasty (221–206 BCE) lasted a very short period before a huge peasant uprising. On this basis, a unified and powerful Han Dynasty appeared. The unified Sui Dynasty was almost as short. Similar to the Qin Dynasty, only two emperors ruled, followed by a huge peasant uprising at the end of the Sui Dynasty. On this basis, a unified and powerful Tang Dynasty came into being. History, of course, does not completely repeat itself. The latter undoubtedly developed towards a more mature peak. Both the Han and Tang Dynasties belong to the rising stage in the development of feudal society and can be called the "dynasties of prosperity". However, why was poetry, the best representative of Chinese feudal society, so neglected and unfruitful in the Han Dynasty that it even lacked a well-established poet? That situation continued until the Jian'an era, which is the end of the Han Dynasty and the beginning of 400 years of wars and raids. Is reviewing the development of history and poetry not enough to arouse people's deep thinking? The following text describes the difficulty in reaching the peak of the Tang poetry, and how we should cherish it, in addition to introducing the noticeable symbols in this peak.

I Growth and decline of poetry and *fu*

Azure Stream Poetic Remarks: Poetry Review No. 8 by Yan Yu asks: "Why is the Tang poetry better than the Song poetry? The Tang Dynasty selects scholar-officials via poetry, so there are many specialised studies. That is why our poetry is inferior". However, his argument is actually not trustworthy. In *Remarks on the Realm of Art and Literature*, Wang Shizhen says,

> People said that the Tang poetry is especially exquisite because the Tang Dynasty selects scholar-officials via poetry, but it is not true. There are few excellent poems composed in the provincial examinations. Top poems such as "Xiang Spirits" by Qian Qi are only one out of a hundred million.

In fact, the Song Dynasty also "selected scholar-officials via poetry". *Encyclopaedia of Classics, Reports and Remarks: Volume 30* reads:

> The civil examination office in the Department of Rites selected Presented Scholars (also *Jinshi*) in the Song Dynasty,... The names of those successful candidates were listed in the Department of National Affairs. Every candidate has to write a poem, a *fu*, an essay, five political discourses, ten completions of context in the *Analects of Confucius*, ten argumentations on the excerpts in *Spring and Autumn* or *Book of Rites*.

In the Song Dynasty, poetry and *fu* are also tested, but why is the Song poetry inferior to the Tang poetry? Obviously, the key problem is not about selecting scholar-officials via poetry. Besides, poetry and *fu* are listed with essays, following the old means of selecting scholar-officials in the Tang Dynasty. It shows that poetry is not the key in examinations. Aiming to select officials, the ancient examination system does not focus on poetry, *fu*, or essays. *Tang Decrees and Regulations: Volume 76* reads:

> In the ninth month of the 22nd year of Zhenguan, the Examination Councillor Wang Shidan was responsible for the selection. At that time, candidates Zhang Changling and Wang Gongjin, brilliant talents, were famous in the capital. However, Shidan gave low evaluations to their literary and political discourses. The whole court did not know the reason. When it was reported to the throne, Emperor Taizong was surprised that the name list did not include Changling, etc. Thus, Shidan was summoned to explain it. Shidan answered, "These candidates indeed have literary talents, but their style is light and frivolous, and they will never become superior talents. If I promoted them, I am afraid that young generations would follow suit and change the elegant style of Your Majesty. The emperor took the answer as a perceptive remark, and later Shidan was proven right.

44 *Symbols at the peak of the Tang poetry*

This can explain the original intention of scholar-officials selection in the Tang Dynasty. In the same volume of *Tang Decrees and Regulations*, it also states:

> In the fourth month of the second year of Tiaolu (679–680), Liu Sili was appointed as the Examination Councillor. At first, *Jinshi* candidates only attended the test of political discourses. Considering it commonplace and simple, Sili suggested that the throne test candidates on the completion of context in classics and essay writing. After that, it became customary.

"The test of political discourses" is the key, while "essay writing" is randomly added by the Examination Councillor. Since it is complementary, it is subject to change. In the same volume of *Tang Decrees and Regulations*, it states:

> In the tenth month of the second year of Jianzhong (780–783), Quan Zhi, an Imperial Secretary, and Zhao Zan, a Civil Examination Officer in the Department of Rites, reported to the throne that *Jinshi* candidates have to test a poem and *fu*, five discourses on the current situation and three discourses on understanding classics. It's suggested that a type of didactic literary composition, an argumentation, a report to the throne, and a literary eulogy should be used to take the place of poetry and *fu*; however, two political discourses should still be tested.

An article in the tenth month of the eighth year of Taihe (827–835) in the same volume of *Tang Decrees and Regulations* reads:

> The Department of Rites reported: since the beginning of the dynasty, the civil examinations at the provincial and state levels have been testing poetry and *fu*, completions of context in classics, and five political discourses. There were temporary changes occasionally, but the exams resumed shortly.

If these are the evidence of "selecting scholar-officials via poetry", the exact statement should be "selecting scholar-officials via poetry and *fu*". If we can explain why the Tang poetry flourished with "selecting scholar-officials via poetry and *fu*", how can we use the same reason to explain why *fu* experienced a setback in the Tang Dynasty? The two cannot thrive at the same time, I think. Of course, I do not mean that no one wrote *fu* in the Tang Dynasty. Since it was often one of the test subjects, how did no one write in this form? It just means that there were no excellent works. This is just like the fact that there were few excellent longer five-character regulated poems in the Tang Dynasty even though this form was tested as an examination

Symbols at the peak of the Tang poetry 45

subject. The growth and decline of literary genres are due to both social conditions and internal laws. "The Han *fu*" and "the Tang poetry" respectively represent such similar unified eras of prosperity in the Han and Tang Dynasties, but between the two there is great incompatibility. In the Han Dynasty, there were writers of *fu* but no masters of poetry, while in the Tang Dynasty, there were poets but no masters of *fu*. In the middle, the Wei, Jin, and Six Dynasties witnessed the coexistence of poetry and *fu*, showing a transitional compromise. Isn't this also an objective phenomenon worthy of attention? This phenomenon can show us that the five- and seven-character poetry from Jian'an through the Six Dynasties was at a stage of transition and compromise towards its maturity and peak. At this stage, poetry began to dominate, and *fu* began to deviate from the style of the Han *fu*, and gradually drew close to poetry. Right before the Sui and Tang Dynasties, there appeared in Yu Xin's (513–581) *fu* a few compositions that could be called poems, such as "*Fu* to Candles":

> In frontiers Dragon Sand and Wild Geese, armours are cool.
> In Mount Heaven with no moon, guards only have clothes thin.
> To hang clothes, I'm afraid a lantern is too dim;
> To thread a needle is hardest under the moon.

"*Fu* to the Spring" reads:

> Spring has come back to the Garden of Spring.
> In the Hall of Fragrance spring clothes are made.
> Birds in the New Year sing in a thousand ways
> Among willow catkins in the second month.
> When Heyang county is full of flowers,
> The Golden Valley is always filled with trees.
> A clump of fragrant grass makes people stay; /
> A few feet of silk floats across the way.

How different are the two *fu* from seven-character poems? Since the *fu* no longer preserved its own characteristics, there was little need to continue to exist. Then, poetry replaced *fu* without any extra effort. This process of development marks the maturity of classical poetry represented by the five- and seven-character poetry, and shows the path followed by classical Chinese poetry.

The distinction between *fu* and poetry is quite clear in Lu Ji's (188–219) *A Fu on Literature*: "Poetry is exquisite in expressing feelings, and *fu* is distinct in describing things". Although *fu* and poetry are rhymed in the original Chinese, their functions are obviously different. *Fu* is mainly about the description of things, while poetry is mainly for the expression of feelings, which is its most essential feature beyond the reach of other genres.

46 *Symbols at the peak of the Tang poetry*

From the very beginning, classical Chinese poetry embarked on the most favourable path with respect for its development, thus achieving the greatest success, and making China always proud of its poetry. The description of things is not a speciality of poetry; to be exact, it is the speciality of prose. *Fu* is, therefore, a genre between poetry and prose, with the form of end rhymes in poetry and some special features of prose. Therefore, *The Literary Mind and the Carving of Dragons: Explanation on Fu* defines *fu* as focused on description. The language of poetry is known for its refinement, while the language of prose is best for description and narration. *Fu* is mainly concerned with description and narration, but it can't be as wide-ranging as prose. Influence by *fu*, *pianwen*[1] appeared in the Six Dynasties. But once the Tang poetry took the position of *fu*, the Tang proses replaced parallel *pianwen*. How similar are the two styles' fates! Thus, the decline of *fu* and its influence have become a clear symbol of the complete maturity of poetry.

The name of *fu* is first found in Xun Qing's five works, namely, "*Fu* on Rites", "*Fu* on Intelligence", "*Fu* on the Cloud", "*Fu* on the Silkworm", and "*Fu* on Didactic Literary Compositions". They are constructed on the dialogues between attending ministers and the emperor. This pattern has been playing a role in the *fu* in the Han Dynasty and even the Six Dynasties, as shown in "*Fu* on the Snow" and "*Fu* on the Moon". Thus, *fu* traditionally bears the interest of the imperial court. Of course, there are palace poetry and ordered poetry, but they obviously do not belong to the orthodoxy, just as feeling-expression *fu* is not in the orthodoxy of *fu*. Palace poetry is actually *fu* in poetry, and its extravagant ornateness and emphasis on the description are the characteristics of *fu*. When *fu* in the Six Dynasties drew close to poetry, it also influenced poetry. All these are the compromises at the transitional stages. Therefore, the five- and seven-character poetry circle had a tortuous maturity process.

At last, poetry reached its peak of prosperity after it completely replaced *fu* and *pianwen* that are under the influence of *fu*. At that time, the final position for *fu* and its influence were only kept in the civil examinations for scholar-officials, because longer five-character regulated poetry is also a kind of *fu* in poetry. Then, "selecting scholar-officials via poetry and *fu*" could have benefited only the prosperity of *fu* and *pianwen*. How can it be the reason for the prosperity of the Tang poetry? However, it helps us to understand the relationship of growth and decline between poetry and *fu*.

We can say that one of the symbols of the prosperity of poetry is the decline of *fu*, which is exactly the same as the decline of palace poetry, after which the Tang poetry completely reached the peak of maturity.

---

1 *Pianwen*, or parallel prose, is a kind of rhythmical prose characterised by parallelism, antithesis, and ornateness, popular in the Southern and Northern Dynasties.

II Quatrains' emergence in the poetry circle

When the Tang poetry reached its pinnacle, the characteristics of poetry were closer to natural expression, which shows its artistic authenticity and simplicity, and the true liberation of language. Since the Jian'an era, poetry had moved away from the tradition of songs, but then returned to it. Because *fu* is "recited without an accompanying song", then is not the decline of *fu* another proof of the revival of songs? Therefore, the emergence of quatrains became a new breakthrough in poetry. The poems sung in the Tang Dynasty were mainly quatrains. *Collection of Special Stories* by Xue Yongruo of Tang recorded a story of wall drawing in an official residence:

> After a while, a singer clapped her bamboo boards and sang: "When cold rain came to River Wu at night, / I bid farewell at Mount Chu alone at dawn. / If my friends in Luoyang ask about me: / A piece of ice heart is in a jade pot". Changling drew on the wall and said, "One quatrain of mine". After a while, another singer sang: "Case opened, tears fall down my chest / At your letter written the other day. / How lonely the Night Terrace seems, / But a scholar like Ziyun rests here". Gao Shi drew on the wall and said, "One quatrain of mine"...

In fact, the quatrain written by Gao Shi is the first four lines in "Crying for Liang the Ninth, Privy Treasurer of Shanfu" (see *Anthology of Poems: Spirit of Mountains and Rivers*). However, it was sung as a single quatrain, showing that quatrains are most suitable for singing. Quatrains originated as folk songs and extensively appeared in the folk songs in the Southern and Northern Dynasties, but few poets had such writings. It is not until the peak of the Tang poetry that quatrains became the most active form of expression in the poetry circle. Zhang Ruoxu is famous for his poem "Spring River Flowery Moonlit Night", which is especially fresh and lively because it is actually composed of nine quatrains. "Spring River Flowery Moonlit Night" belongs to the "Wu Songs" of the Southern Dynasties, which are originally quatrains of folk songs. Therefore, in this poem, Zhang Ruoxu changed rhymes every four lines, and the whole poem has several rhythmic variations as if the melody is slowly emerging. From the moonrise to the moonset, it intermittently forms a long lyrical poem. Moreover, its continuous changes of rhyme every four lines make it more natural to reveal its leaping nature, which is a basic characteristic of poetic language, though sometimes vague and sometimes obvious. The abundance and freedom of the leaping nature are manifestations of the full maturity of poetic language and the richness of poetic lyricism. Such lines as "A hundred poems for a barrel of wine" are only achievable in such a mature poetic era. If the ancient five-character poems since Jian'an unavoidably have considerable prose elements, then quatrains require the poetic language to be more purified; the emergence of quatrains in the poetry circle can be considered another distinct symbol

48 *Symbols at the peak of the Tang poetry*

of the full maturity of five- and seven-character poems. Seven-character ancient poems of the Tang people are relatively more active than five-character ancient poems because sometimes the latter are unavoidably accustomed to the established transitional expressions, while the former are brand-new. Seven-character ancient poems, like quatrains, suddenly became people's favourite at the height of the High Tang poetry. While five-character ancient poems have few changes of rhymes, seven-character ancient poems are constantly changing their rhymes. For example, consider Li Qi's "Ancient Army March":

> In the day, they climb up mounts to watch beacon fire;
> At dusk, they water horses by the Jiaohe River.
> In the dark, sandy wind, people remain on the go.
> *Pipa* plays for the princess are full of sorrow.
> Wild clouds of thousands of li see no towns in sight.
> Relentless rain and snow fall on the endless sand.
> The moaning geese are flying through the sky each night.
> Soldiers are also shedding tears in the Hu tribe's land.
> Hearing that the Jade Gate Fortress has been blocked,
> They must follow the chariot to fight without fear.
> Bones of warriors are buried in the wild each year;
> They see grapes sent to the Hans until overstocked.

In the 12 lines, the rhyming scheme of the original Chinese poem changes three times, actually forming three quatrains. Seven-character ancient poems such as Cao Pi's "Song of the Yan" and Bao Zhao's (c. 414–466) "The Roads are Hard: An Imitation" originated as a song, and they have the same rhythm with quatrains in the musical tradition. Like quatrains, seven-character ancient poems had existed from ancient times before the Tang Dynasty. However, they had not fully come into view until the peak of the Tang poetry. Is it only accidental?

Regulated poetry, evolving from longer regulated poems, is also a kind of poetic genre formed towards the peak of the Tang poetry. Its level and oblique (also *pingze*) rhythm also evolved from the "description of dissonant sounds" in longer five-character regulated poems. It had no origin in folk songs and could not be used for singing; but in its evolution, it embarked on the path of simplification and plainness; it changed the tedious "four tones and eight dissonances" into a simple and easy level and oblique rhythm, and turned the tedious parallel structures into only eight lines in each poem, only requiring the middle four lines to have parallelism and antithesis, which greatly improved the refinement of poetic language. As a special feature of the Chinese language, parallelism and antithesis are natural in poems. Antithetical lines often appear in seven-character ancient poems and occasionally in quatrains. What matters is whether the expression is natural

Symbols at the peak of the Tang poetry   49

or not. We cannot help asking by what force regulated poetry can break through the influence of longer five-character regulated poetry to achieve its own evolution and reform since the latter is a designated poetic form in "selecting scholar-officials via poetry and *fu*". The answer can only be that the great wave of natural expression in the poetry circle provided the liberatory power. Therefore, regulated poems are much more refined and vivid than longer ones. This is exactly in line with the characteristics of quatrains and seven-character ancient poems. Cui Hao wrote one of the most famous seven-character regulated poems, "Yellow Crane Tower":

> The immortal has flown away on the yellow crane,
> Leaving here an empty Yellow Crane Tower to date.
> The yellow crane has gone and never comes again.
> For a thousand years, only the white clouds await.
> Trees at the Hanyang town stand by the shining shore;
> The Parrot sandbar has grass in the lush, green state.
> After sunset, where can I find my home of yore?
> The misty Yangtze River brings me longing great.

The vivid and lyric qualities of this poem made it one of the masterpieces of regulated poetry; although its first four lines do not fully conform to the level and oblique rhythm or the strict requirement of parallelism and antithesis, it is still recognised as the representative work of seven-character regulated poetry. Obviously, Li Bai's poems such as "The Parrot Sandbar" and "Mounting the Phoenix Terrace at Jinling" deliberately imitated it. Then, what is the prominent feature of its writing? In the first four lines, three phrases of "yellow crane" are used in one breath, speeding up the pace of the regulated poem that is slowed down by the parallelism and antithesis, thus contributing to the unrestrained poetic feelings. This is an anomaly in regulated poetry. The succession of the three phrases of "yellow crane" naturally makes the first four lines form a prominent melody, and the following four lines are naturally a leap; therefore, the "Yellow Crane Tower" seems to be a seven-character ancient poem in regulated poetry. Such an outstanding poem stands at the top of seven-character regulated poetry, even though it is not exactly a regulated poem, but somewhat like a seven-character ancient poem. Is it not worthy of our attention? What does it suggest here? It suggests that the peak of the whole poetry circle is based on the spontaneous flow of emotions in quatrains and seven-character ancient poems. The emancipated language, unrestrained sentiment, fresh melody, and heroic lyric constituted the most distinctive style of the Tang poetry. It is through this power that regulated poetry is freed from longer regulated poetry and becomes more vivid and natural. The so-called "The lotus comes out of clear water, / And is decorated with Nature" (Li Bai: "On my Exile to Yelang at the Emperor's Order after Chaotic Wars, I Miss my Old Friends and Express my Feelings:

50 *Symbols at the peak of the Tang poetry*

To Jiangxia Governor Wei Liangzai", often shortened as "To Jiangxia Governor Wei Liangzai") shows the essence and characteristics of the whole Tang poetry. Therefore, regulated poetry can be completely liberated from the decorative longer regulated poetry.

Quatrains, seven-character ancient poems, and regulated poems are novelties at the height of the Tang poetry. Although the shortest, quatrains are the most vigorous, the closest to songs, the most distinct from prose, and mostly "naturally decorated". Its appearance in the poetry circle means that the poetic language is completely mature, authentic, and plain. It is the most distinctive pearl and the most prominent symbol at the peak of the Tang poetry.

III The heroic feeling in frontier fortress poetry

The maturity of poetic language is inseparable from the spiritual outlook of the time. However, it has its internal laws, and has to go through a tortuous process of development; the authenticity and simplicity of the Tang poetry do not necessarily mean total simplicity. Eliciting profundity out of simplicity is never simple. Without the development of the 400 years in the poetry circle since Jian'an, the language of the Tang poetry would not have been mature at once. However, the conditions of the time determine whether the poetic language is mature enough and how fast it becomes mature. Without the vigorous spirit of the Tang Dynasty, it is unavoidable to ask how much achievement the five- and seven-character poetry could have made and whether quatrains would have been so popular in the poetry circle. "The High Tang Voice" suddenly burst out in the spring garden of poetry, growing into gorgeous and exotic flowers and fruits, which are the products of the maturity of the poetic language itself and of social development in the Tang Dynasty. The convergence of these two maturities and developments produced the peak of the Tang poetry, which is unprecedented in the classical poetry circle for its magnificence and high-spirited atmosphere. In this unprecedented and unsurpassed poetry circle, there appeared a remarkable singing, frontier fortress poetry.

The themes of the Tang poetry are very extensive, and the frontier fortress is only one of them. It is especially noteworthy because it seems to belong only to the High Tang. Before the Tang Dynasty, it was rare, and it almost disappeared after the High Tang. Li Yi is almost the last poet to write frontier fortress poems. But precisely the High Tang had the most untroubled times on the frontier fortress. Therefore, the main purpose of frontier fortress poems was not to write about wars, but a kind of frontier defence song full of heroic spirit in a relatively peaceful environment. In the fourth year of Zhenguan under the rule of Emperor Taizong, the Eastern Turks were defeated, and the remnants were incorporated. In the ninth year of Zhenguan, the Turpan was defeated. Then, the situation on the frontier was basically stabilised, and became more moderate in the Kaiyuan era. Moreover, in the 100 years of prosperity and development of the Tang society, its national

Symbols at the peak of the Tang poetry 51

strength rose to a peak and earned itself more prestige on the frontier defence; thus it seized the chance to live peacefully as a matter of fact. The frontier fortress poems were written in such conditions. After the An Shi Rebellion, the peace of the frontier defence was like a dying yellow flower, and frontier fortress poems became the past in the wake of the Tang Dynasty's faded prosperity. Frontier fortress poems belong to the Tang Dynasty only, so they have the characteristics of the time and become the most distinctive symbol at the peak of poetry. Wang Changling's "Army March" No. 5 reads:

At dusk, dusty and windy is the great desert.
All red flags half-furled, we ride out of the camp gate.
Front army fought north of the Tao River at night,
Declaring they captured Tuyu Hun the Chief alive.

The poem illustrates the strong power of border defence, without which no peace is possible on the frontier fortress. "Fortress Song" No. 2 also says:

I water my horse and cross the river
In autumn, water cold and wind sword-like.
In the vast desert, the sun has not set,
And Lintao is seen far away in dark.
About the fierce battle of the Great Wall,
All border guards talk with a high spirit.
Since ancient till now, in the yellow dust
Lots of white bones are cluttered with wild weeds.

It shows that war is cruel. Although "All border guards talk with a high spirit", it is a historical tragedy that "Since ancient till now, in the yellow dust, / Lots of white bones are cluttered with wild weeds". This further explains that the nature of frontier defence is to ensure peace, but not to wage wars. This is almost a common understanding in the frontier fortress poems of the Tang Dynasty, and it is more than just about the Tao River area. Therefore, Li Bai states in "Fighting in the City South" that "Now we know soldiers are weapons; / The sage would never use them if not necessary". Du Fu also remarks in "Out of the Fortress: Former" that "As long as it stops invasion, / Meaningless is to kill more people"! It is precisely on the basis of this universal understanding of war and peace that the Kaiyuan era had the rarest wars and the most stable peace, and became the cradle of frontier fortress poetry.

Wang Changling's two poems are actually historical summaries. In the Kaiyuan era, Tuyu Hun has already fled to Tubo, the Tibetan regime. Thus, it is certainly not about a battle at that time; of course, "the fierce battle of the Great Wall" is also a historical summary just as "In the passes of Han under the moon from Qin" shows. Therefore, the frontier fortress poems of the Tang Dynasty are often not about a specific battle, time, and place, but the singing of the frontier fortress as a whole in a wide range of time

52   *Symbols at the peak of the Tang poetry*

and space. So the attraction of frontier fortress poetry lies not in a specific battlefield or battle; but mainly in a kind of solemn and heroic feeling, an exotic sentiment, a broad vision, and the confidence in the frontier defence. Its specific content is often an expansion of the traditional theme of wanderers, political vision, as well as landscape and scenery. In fact, Li Bai's "I am willing to assist in governing the empire, making it peaceful and united with all the seas and counties" ("A Complaint to Privy Treasurer Meng on Behalf of Shoushan") is precisely the lofty political ideal including the stability of the frontier fortress; thus Li Bai is said to have written "Answers to the Tibetans". Wang Wei's "Song of Youth" reads, "Who knows not the great pain in the frontier? / Though killed, the bones still smell brave without fear". This is the spiritual outlook of the High Tang. At this time, the theme of wanderers includes not only visiting officials, but military servicemen. Wang Changling's "Boudoir Complaint" thus reads:

A young wife in her boudoir knew no grief.
In spring, she made up to mount a tower green.
Seeing willows by the roadside, she'd blame
Herself for urging her husband for wealth and fame.

Li Guinian's singing of Wang Wei's quatrain "Song of Yizhou" states:

In the moonlit wind, yearnings me attack.
You've been in force for more than ten years.
The day you went, I advised you in tears
To send me more letters when geese come back.

In the ancient poem, the "wanderer" became a soldier "in force". Moreover, Li Bai's "Always in Yearning" also says: "No one would bring you this song full of sad longing. / How I wish the spring breeze to Yanran would it bring!" These lines show that the life at the frontier fortress has gone deep into the ordinary life, that is to say, the heroic feeling in the frontier fortress is in harmony with that of the ordinary life. The singing of the frontier fortress found the most appropriate occasion for the expression of this heroic feeling; it stirred up the heroic feeling of the time and was established on it. Just as the confidence of the frontier defence is based on the prosperity of social development, so is the heroic feeling of the frontier defence based on confidence in daily life. Without the High Tang, there would never have existed the frontier fortress poems. Without the ubiquitous vigour of life, the frontier fortress scenery would have long been drowned out by the desolate and monotonous sandstorms. Thus Wang Wei says:

In the vast desert a lone smoke rises up;
In the long river, the setting sun is full.

—"Envoy to the Fortress"

The two lines well describe the scenery of the frontier fortress. Moreover, Wang Wei also writes:

> In sunset, the river and lake are white;
> When the tide comes, the sky and earth are blue.
> —"Seeing off Xing, Governor of Guizhou"

> The Hanjiang River flows out of the sky;
> The mount colours are hidden in the mist.
> —"The Hanjiang River View"

Are not the clear vision and broad mind comparable to the former poems? Wang Wei's landscape poems cannot be represented only by such lines far away from the human world as "In my later years, I was quiet, / And I didn't care about anything". His vigorous youthful spirit in his early years is vividly shown in:

> The New Home wine worth ten thousand is so mellow,
> Enticing young roaming swordsmen in Xianyang town.
> They drink heartily to their spirit and renown,
> Leaving their steeds by a high inn to weeping willows.
> —"Song of Youth" No. 1

Without such a state of mind, there would not have existed landscape poems like "In sunset, the rivers and lakes are white. / When the tide comes, the sky and water are blue", nor would there have been frontier fortress poems like "In the vast desert a lone smoke rises up; / In the long river the setting sun is full". Frontier fortress scenery is actually a test of the heroic feeling in that era. In Gao Shi's "Farewell to Brother Dong" No. 1, we read:

> White sun dimmed by yellow clouds vast,
> Geese flew in wind, snow overcast.
> Though bosom friends ahead are few,
> Who in the world never knows you?

Without such strong confidence in life, what scenery can be appreciated under such vast yellow clouds and chilly north wind? Why did the singing of these scenes disappear right after the peak of the High Tang? It is because the emergence of frontier fortress poetry was the product of the spirit of the era. The clear vision and unrestrained heroic feeling reflected the striding footsteps of the entire era, which is one of the characteristics of "the High Tang Voice" praised in the following dynasties. In frontier fortress poetry, the seven-character quatrains and seven-character ancient poems are the best. The relationship between the two has been described before. From Wang Changling to Li Yi, the seven-character quatrains singing of

54 *Symbols at the peak of the Tang poetry*

the frontier fortress once again proved the broad prospects of quatrains. The role of seven-character poetry in the whole peak of the Tang poetry is especially evident now. The complete maturity of five- and seven-character poems as a whole is actually marked by the maturity of seven-character poetry. These are the embodiment of not only the development of poetic language itself but also the spirit of the time. Frontier fortress poetry can exactly describe the flesh and blood relationship between them.

The artistic attainments, and the brilliant and abundant achievements of the Tang poetry are inspiring us to understand the peak of poetry in many ways.

Originally published in *Social Science Front*, 1982 (4)

4 How did landscape poetry come into being?

Landscape poetry is an inevitable occurrence in the development of poetry. In recognising and transforming Nature, human beings have been objectifying it, which is inevitably reflected in poetry. At first, such objectification appeared in the form of mythology. With the development of productive forces, the era of mythology passed away, and Nature naturally became an important aspect of the rich imagination in poetry. Foreshadowing (or *qixing*), the writing technique of introducing the subject by mentioning other things first, is used many times in "Airs of the States" and "Minor Court Hymns":

> Of yore I went away,
> Willows would not say bye.
> Missing, I'm here today;
> Both rain and snow come by.

This kind of work indisputably proves the above idea. But the pre-Qin Dynasty is only a beginning; from *Chuci*, we can clearly see the last light of mythology, and its interaction with the fresh charm of the natural landscape. How much brilliance would have been lost, if Qu Yuan removed the landscape description in "Nine Songs"!

> Gentle is the autumn wind;
> The Dongting Lake ripples with the falling leaves.

How fresh and touching the poetic lines are! If we quote Karl Marx's famous saying that "man creates beauty according to the laws of beauty" in poetry writing, then the appearance of natural beauty in poetry is not subject to people's will, but subject to an objective and inevitable development. When productive forces developed to a certain period, especially with the maturity of feudal society dependent on agricultural production, the transformation of Nature became more common. The era of gods passed away, and people were mainly living close to Nature. These are the favourable conditions for the development of landscape poetry.

56 *How did landscape poetry come into being?*

The feudal society and culture of ancient Chinese are far more developed than those of other nationalities around the world, and so is landscape poetry. Is it only a coincidence? Poetry, as the main literary form in ancient Chinese feudal society, matured early, and relied on natural scenes more than stories and plots to enrich its imagination. Since the Yuanjia period (424–453) of the Song of the Southern Dynasties, a large number of landscape poems have emerged prominently, making the expressions of poetry more diverse, which played an important role in promoting and enriching the artistry of the Tang poetry. In Du Fu's words:

> Country broken, mountains and rivers remain.
> In the spring, grass and trees grow green in vain.
> Feeling the time, flowers make me shed tears.
> Hating farewell, my heart flying birds fears.[1]

Here "mountains and rivers", "grass and trees", "flowers", and "birds" have become a deeper revelation of the inner world. Without landscape poetry as a basis, there would have not been such poetic lines. Other examples are: "Green, green is the grass on the plain, / Growing, dying year after year. / A wild fire burns it but in vain / As spring breeze helps it grow again",[2] "You left at Pavilion Baling; / The Bashui water was surging; / Above the river, ancient trees grow without flowers, / While the sad spring grass below has a broken heart".[3] The rich imagination cannot appear without the achievements of landscape poetry. Like mythology, landscape poetry is close to an artistic form. The good and the bad are intermingled in mythology, and the same can be said of landscape poetry. However, mythology and landscape poetry are generally beautiful and lovely, because they reflect the liveliness and infinite richness of human imagination. Mythology is often not simply about gods, because gods often interact with people. Likewise, landscape poetry is seldom about a simple natural scenery, because the landscape is also often connected to people. Perhaps some people will say that landscape poetry related to humans is not true landscape poetry, and then very few works can be regarded as landscape poetry. If we separate landscape poetry from palace poetry, then how many poems were purely describing natural scenery even in the Southern Dynasties when landscape poetry was created in large quantities?

The theme of love is embodied in Jiangnan folk songs such as "Songs of Wu", "Songs of Jiangling", "Songs of Worship", and "A Song of the Western Islet". Most of the literati's works are concerned with political aspiration, lives of travelling official, wanderers, travels, and home thoughts—as shown

---

1 Du Fu. "Spring View".
2 Bai Juyi. "A Farewell Poem on the Old Plain Grass".
3 Li Bai. "Farewell at Baling".

How did landscape poetry come into being? 57

in "The sunset spreads out like a colourful brocade; / The clean river is as quiet as a white silk", "At the skyline, a returning boat is visible. / In the cloudy mist, trees along the river are seen",[4] "The quiet river may have billows, / But your lonely boat must move on",[5] and "On the dark river the rain will come. / The early wind turns the waves white".[6] These most representative landscape poems are not only about natural sceneries. In the northern songs, there appeared lines such as "By the Yellow River at Ford Meng, / The green willows wave goodbye", and "Chile Steppe, under Mount Yin...".[7] Do they have nothing to do with the flourishing of landscape poetry in the Southern Dynasties? Indeed, landscape poetry thrived in the Southern Dynasties with its economic development, neither for the official-scholars' preference of gardens since the Wei and Jin Dynasties, nor for the hermits' escape from reality into caves. Of course, landscape poetry as an artistic form can be used to write about gardens or hermit lives. Nevertheless, the actual development of landscape poetry has not much to do with gardens or seclusion. The landscape sceneries in the poems are not originally from the Wei, Jin, and Six Dynasties, but from ancient times, though limited in number. After *Shijing* and *Chuci*, we read "At Jiangnan Lotuses are Wayside" in the Han *yuefu* ballads:

> At Jiangnan lotuses are wayside.
> Green foliage overlaps one another;
> Fish are playing under the leaves.
> Fish under the leaves east,
> Fish under the leaves west,
> Fish under the leaves south,
> Fish under the leaves north.

This can be regarded as a representative landscape poem. However, later scholars' works, of which Cao Cao's "Watching the Vast Sea" was generally recognised as an early representative, were about neither gardens nor seclusion. The poetry about gardens and seclusion flourished since the Wei and Jin Dynasties, while landscape poetry did not make greater progress or more achievements than others, especially in the poems mainly about gardens and seclusion. It was not until the Liang and Chen (557–589) Dynasties when palace poetry flourished that there appeared more ordered poems mainly about the courtyard landscape, which are similar to garden poems, but a little later than landscape poems. Before the prosperity of landscape poetry, metaphysical poetry had monopolised the poetry circle for nearly

---

4 Xie Tiao. "Climbing the Three Peaks after Sunset to Look at the Capital" and "Arriving at Xuancheng County from New Forest Ford to Bridge Ford".

5 Yin Keng. "Reply to Mr Fu: Returning to Xiangzhou at Yearend".

6 He Xun. "Farewell".

7 "Song of Plucking Willows" and "Song of Chile".

58 *How did landscape poetry come into being?*

a hundred years, which might as well be more directly related to the escape from reality. However, landscape and sceneries are especially scarce in those poems. On the contrary, in folk songs based in reality, there are more descriptions of landscape and sceneries at that time; and their new look is quite different from the past, as shown in:

> Spring breeze stirring the heart of spring,
> I look at the mountains and forests,
> Where sceneries are spectacular
> And birds sing gently in the sunshine.[8]
> Jiangling is away from Yangzhou
> For three thousand and three hundred *li*;
> We have travelled thirteen hundred *li*,
> Leaving two thousand *li* untravelled.[9]

Those who escaped from reality did not write about landscape, whereas those who did not were interested in landscape poems. How on earth should this be explained? Landscape poems mainly focused on travelling and sceneries; even Xie Lingyun appeared as a traveller. Whether he is a hermit or not is surely worth research. But anyway, he is different from the hermits since the Wei and Jin Dynasties who lived in secluded places, quiet and inactive. Particularly active, Xie Lingyun travelled around. It is said that Fan Li boating on the Five Lake was also considered a hermit. They somewhat resembled each other, but Fan Li was famous rather as a counsellor. However, *The Literary Mind and the Carving of Dragons: On Poetry* opines that

> The literary singing at the beginning of the Liu Song Dynasty had reformations in genres. Only when the metaphysical poems following Zhuangzi (also Chuang-tzu, 369–286 BCE, a well-known Chinese thinker, philosopher and writer) and Laozi (also Lao Tzu, Lao-tzu, Lao-tse, 604–531 BCE, the founder of Taoism) declined, did landscape poetry begin to develop,

which seems true. That is to say, only when the Zhuang-Lao thought representing the seclusion of the Wei and Jin Dynasties quitted the poetry circle, landscape poetry gained real development. In other words, under the control of Zhuang-Lao thought at that time, it was not conducive to the development of landscape poetry, so the process of reform encountered opposing ideas. Then, is it not enough to describe the disharmonious relationship between the emergence of landscape poetry and the reclusive lives of scholar-officials?

---

8 Songs of Wu. "Miss Midnight's Songs of the Four Seasons: Twenty Songs of Spring" No. 1.
9 Songs of Wu. "Fourteen Songs of Regret" No. 3.

How did landscape poetry come into being? 59

Moreover, even if Xie Lingyun escaped from reality, he was still a hermit because he believes that "Woodcutters and hermits are hidden in mountains, / But for different reasons". Moreover, "digging mountains and dredging lakes", he wrote lines such as "No dust and noise in the garden" and "Once I returned to my old garden",[10] which are related to gardens. However, his large number of landscape poems are not based on seclusion or gardening. This is similar to the fact that Xie Lingyun's landscape poems often have a metaphysical tail, but this tail is not the basis of, but an obstacle to, his landscape poems. Xie Lingyun wrote so many excellent landscape poems because he had got rid of the shackles of metaphysical poetry, ran out of seclusion, and wrote in a style quite different from that of garden poetry. Undoubtedly, in his poems, there are still tails that can't be cut off, and serious demerits of escaping from reality, but do these contribute to his achievements in landscape poetry? On the contrary, because Xie Lingyun has such obvious shortcomings, his achievements in landscape poetry also have very obvious limitations, foremost of which is that emotions can't be interwoven with sceneries as researchers often point out. Nature, as a lyric object, should have emotions interwoven with sceneries. Ever since "Of yore I went away, / Willows would not say bye", emotions and sceneries have been interwoven. Why aren't they interwoven in Xie Lingyun's poems? This is obviously not the problem of landscape poetry, but Xie Lingyun's personal problem. The development of landscape poetry needs not necessarily go through a stage that emotions can't be interwoven with sceneries. However, Xie Lingyun's own shortcomings make the interweaving impossible. His shortcomings are only his own, not belonging to others, as clearly shown in Tao Yuanming before him and Xie Tiao after him.

Xie Lingyun's landscape poems do have their own peculiarities. They seem more objective than ordinary landscape works. He is a bit like a travelling journalist photographing fresh sceneries with exquisite photographic techniques along his way. However, many scenes, even in the same poem, do not seem to have much connection with each other. What are the reasons behind it? In other words, the metaphysical philosophy of the latter half in Xie's poems cannot be unified with the landscape of the first half; thus, not only do the two halves often distinguish as two poems for their fresh or unoriginal style, but the first half of landscape lacks a unified and obvious idea, so they are dissociated as if they are still at the perceptual stage rather than at the stage of complete conceptual understanding. As for the conceptual understanding in the latter half of the metaphysical tail, it is obvious, systematic and inherent, independent of the landscape in the former half. Therefore, the two have certain superficial logic but no inherent connection. If we say that its metaphysical tail considers Nature as a footnote of the abstract metaphysical statement of "Laozi and Zhuangzi understand Nature",

---

10 Xie Lingyun. "Building Fence Along the Rapids in the Tree Garden of the South Field" and "Returning to the Old Garden to Visit Imperial Secretaries Yan and Fan".

60 *How did landscape poetry come into being?*

then it is precisely in the landscape that the same Nature is regarded as an objective, concrete, and changing novelty. These two different attitudes and different views illustrate the clashing worldviews. That is to say, Xie Lingyun's worldview has a systematic and declining ideological system represented by his metaphysical poems; however, it has an unsystematic, close to perceptual, relatively open and healthy new requirement for natural beauty. These phenomena are possible with those people in a declining class who are unwilling to be dejected. On the one hand, the old ideology still clings to him; on the other, he becomes soberer in the face of a sudden decline, trying to struggle out of the dead and decaying remains, breathing fresh air, and absorbing some healthy aesthetic viewpoints. However, as class constraints still hold him firmly, this sobriety can only end there, so his gain is fragmentary, novel but somewhat strange. This forms the unique feature of Xie Lingyun's landscape poetry, though not in all of his poems. In "The bright moon is shining on the snow, / Fresh wind is strong and sorrowful",[11] emotions and sceneries are interwoven.

This can only be applied to most of his more successful landscape poems. However, if he did not have such a will to fight against the decline, nor did he absorb a healthy aesthetic point of view, or if he just wanted to escape into a corner of Nature for the rest of his life without feeling the magnificent changes and fresh forces of Nature, then Xie Lingyun could have only written metaphysical poems, rather than the landscape poems such as "Currents abruptly twist around islets, / And ofttimes rush up river banks", "What's the law of Nature and why? / All things growing are flourishing", and "I touch a trailing plant and listen; / My spring heart belongs to the green cliff".[12] Moreover, there would not have existed in his landscape poems the dissociated state of the two halves as in two different poems; or his landscape poems would have been covered with metaphysical concepts without the beauty of mountains and rivers, similar to the "*Fu* on Visiting Tiantai Mountain" written by Sun Chuo; or emotions and sceneries would have been interwoven into the silence of Zen because he is a Buddhist, as in some of Wang Wei's later poems, which are always unified, not so dissociated as in Xie Lingyun's poems. However, Xie Lingyun, having dissociated from metaphysical poetry and the narrow world of aristocrats, has made new achievements in landscape poetry.

I think if we can distinguish landscape poetry from pastoral poetry (also field and garden poetry) here, it may be helpful to study how landscape poetry came into being and how it developed. In fact, in the period when landscape poems were written in large quantities, there were few rivers, mountains, and fields that belonged purely to the foreworld because they

---

11 Xie Lingyun. "Yearend".
12 Xie Lingyun. "Entering the Pengli Lake Outlet", "Looking afar when Travelling from the South Mountain to the North Mountain Through the Wu Lake", and "A Poem on Passing the White Bank Pavilion".

How did landscape poetry come into being? 61

had been either altered by the broad masses of the people or modified by the ruling class. The former are the mountains and rivers in Nature, while the latter are the gardens and courts built by people. They absorbed the aesthetic views of the working people to varying degrees, and were inevitably transformed according to the interests and preconceptions of the ruling class. These two changes of the natural world are either grand or little, natural or decorative, immense or exquisite, diligent or indulging, infinite or limited, demonstrating different preferences. The former, like life, is infinitely rich, and their development leads to the singing of the country's rivers and mountains, and even the yearning for the frontier fortress, as shown in "Chu fortress adjacent to the Three Xiang, / Mount Jingmen overlooks the nine branches. / The Hanjiang River flows out of the sky; / The mount colours are hidden in the mist", "In the vast desert a lone smoke rises up; / In the long river the setting sun is full",[13] and "Why should the Qiang flute complain of willows? / The spring breeze does not break through the Yumen Pass".[14]

Nevertheless, pastoral poetry embellished the palace poetry because of the former's limitations. Of course, this does not mean that poets cannot write about gardens or sceneries. About gardens are "Verdant grass grows along the river banks; / Green willows in the garden are flourishing",[15] and "In late spring the air is harmonious; / The white sun shines in the garden. / Green willows are like virid strips, / Yellow flowers like scattered gold".[16] "The fine moon falls into the windy woods. / Dew on his clothes, he plays the pure zither. / In the dark, water flowing by the flower path, / Spring stars are shining on the thatched hut"[17] is also undoubtedly a good poem. Natural beauty has its magnificence and changes as well as its quietness and harmony, but it should not be insulated from the beauty in gardens and sceneries. The question is whether it is the starting point or the destination of life, whether it is a prospect or an end, whether it is to strengthen the will of life or to seek excessive pleasures. The scholar-officials' fondness of gardens since the Wei and Jin Dynasties generally belong to the latter.

Pastoral poetry, of course, is somewhat different, depending on whether the main subject is the field or the garden. Tao Yuanming's pastoral poetry can be said to be mainly about the field, and his achievements are beyond the reach of ordinary landscape poetry, but how many poets are like Tao Yuanming? In pastoral poetry in general, the field is just another form of a garden, which we can fully understand if only we are aware that the field of the Paddy Fragrance Village appeared in the Big View Garden. In fact, if a poet can really reveal a little information of the field, he can write good poems. Extremely fresh is the vitality shown in "Level fields embrace the wind

13 Wang Wei. "The Hanjiang River View", "Envoy to the Fortress".
14 Wang Zhihuan. "Song of Liangzhou".
15 "Nineteen Ancient Poems" No. 2.
16 Zhang Han. "Miscellaneous Poems".
17 Du Fu. "An Evening Banquet at Zuo's Manor".

62   *How did landscape poetry come into being?*

afar; / Good seedlings are also flourishing" and "The wind from the south gives / Wings to the new seedlings".[18] In addition, "White water shines outside of the field; / Green peaks stand out of the mountain. / No idle people in the farming month / Since all farm in the South Field"[19] is also a good poem. In most cases, however, a field does not appear with the personality of a field, but with that of a garden. Although the language may be simpler for its involvement with the field, it cannot avoid the fate similar to that of garden poetry, and works of achievements are quite rare.

In the nearly 300 years of the Southern Dynasties, there are not many noteworthy pastoral poems besides those by Tao Yuanming. But landscape poems are quite exceptional and impressive. What an aesthetic kinship exists between "Spring is late, the green wild graceful. / White clouds are gathered on high rocks",[20] "The sound of drums could not be heard, / When the sails were close to the clouds",[21] "The bank flowers blooming near the water, / The river swallows fly around the masts",[22] and folk songs such as "In the second and third months / Grass and water have the same colour", "Over a hundred sailing boats / Are mooring in the River Ford", and "Apes along the Badong Three Gorges cry in sorrow; / Three cries at night make people's clothes stained with tears".[23] These easily seen but excellent works represent the achievements of landscape poetry in the Southern Dynasties, but are far apart from gardens and fields, let alone seclusion. Of course, in reclusive poems, there may be excellent landscape poems since Tao Yuanming is still the "master of reclusive poets". Zuo Si states in his "Poems on the History" the following confrontational lines, "Going out of the palace in coarse clothes, / I follow Xu You to be a hermit, / Tidying my clothes on the high mountain / And washing my feet in the long river". In his successful poem "Inviting Recluses", he also writes that

> White clouds stop at the shady mounds; / Red flowers grow in the sunny woods. / The spring is washing jade-like stones, / Where fishes of fine scales are swimming. / Without silk and bamboo instruments, / The water in the hill makes clear noises. / When people feel like whistling a song, / The bushes will chant by itself in grief.

It depends on whether the seclusion is mainly confronting reality or escaping from it. Here, we recommend some landscape poems in the Southern Dynasties, one group related to gardens and seclusion, and the other related to politics, travelling officials, soldiers on expedition, and travels, to see

---

18 Tao Yuanming. "Two Poems Missing Old Pastoral Cottages in the Early Spring of the Year of the Tenth Rabbit" No. 2, and "Fortune".
19 Wang Wei. "An Evening View after a New Sunny Day".
20 Xie Lingyun. "Entering Pengli Lake Outlet".
21 Yin Keng. "Late in Seeing off Liu Guanglu at a River Ford".
22 He Xun. "To Old Travel Friends".
23 Songs of Jiangling. "Miss Mengzhu", "Music of Stone City", and "Daughters".

which group is more representative of the achievements of landscape poems. I believe the result is not difficult to predict, and obviously there would be a wide gap. This shows that gardens or seclusion do not play an important role in the wide range of landscape poetry, and excellent landscape poems seldom appear there. In the final analysis, theory has to be tested in practice. Is it the landscape poems of outstanding achievement or those of little achievement that have promoted the emergence and development of landscape poetry? This research just wants to illustrate the fact that seclusion, just as gardens, did not play many roles in developing landscape poetry in the Southern Dynasties. On the contrary, it can be said that the development of landscape poetry has increased the vitality of seclusion and gardens. Isn't it Xie Lingyun who has such good lines "In the pond grows spring grass. / In garden willows birds are singing"?

Then, how did landscape poetry come into being? I think, first of all, it should be admitted that a kind of imagery thinking is inevitable for the diverse expression and rich imagination of poetry. However, its emergence must be dependent on the development of economy and waterway transportation in the Southern Dynasties. How come "the literary singing at the beginning of the Liu Song Dynasty had reformations in genres"? This is inseparable from the developing economic maturity in the Yuanjia period of the Liu Song Dynasty. Mr Fan Wenlan states in his book *A Concise General History of China* (Revised edition, Volume II, 371–373):

> Poor in his childhood, Liu Yu had no books to read. He ploughed arable land for a living, and worked as a woodcutter, fisherman, and peddler of shoes... Later, he accumulated war achievements and laid the foundation for the imperial kingdom, which is completely different from the enthroning of Emperor Yuan of the Jin Dynasty who relied on the support of great families. In the Liu Song Dynasty founded by Liu Yu, the Emperor with undivided power was mainly assisted by humble families. The former great families could only be high-ranking officials with little power, hardly trusted by the Emperor. The weakening of the political power of the gentry and the centralization of the Emperor's autocracy made the unification of the Liu Song Dynasty far better than that in the Eastern Jin Dynasty (317–420) with strong separatist regimes... In 424, Emperor Wen of the Liu Song Dynasty ascended the throne. In the 30 years of his rule, the Yangtze River Basin had unprecedented prosperity since the Eastern Jin Dynasty. The development of the southern economy and culture did not really begin until the Yuanjia period under his reign.

The objective reality of the beautiful scenery and fertile land in Jiangnan makes possible the aforementioned works such as "Nine Songs" and "At Jiangnan Lotuses are Wayside". However, in the past, Jiangnan, with backward agricultural technology, insufficient labour force, and undercultivated

64 *How did landscape poetry come into being?*

land, was far away from the economic, political, and cultural centre. It was not fundamentally changed until the regime of Central Plains moved south at the end of the Western Jin Dynasty. It has been more than 100 years since then, and about half a century since Liu Yu took the throne until the Yuanjia period. The political enlightenment ensured more economic development, and it became a truly active and prosperous period, which can be seen from the fact that Jiangnan has become a national granary since the Sui and Tang Dynasties. The business in Jiangnan was also greatly developed on this foundation. Ancient Chinese people's understanding and transformation of Nature, including waterway transportation, reached a new stage. In this development process, it also provided a solid foundation for people to understand the beauty of Nature, which was first expressed in Jiangnan folk songs. Since his ruling, Liu Yu had weakened the monopoly of the clans to a certain extent, and the long-term monopoly of the poetry circle had initially shaken off the heavy pressure of lethargy. All these were still slow, but undoubtedly improved; so the writers created many poems after folk songs, and at the same time lived their lives as travelling officials and visited innumerable mountains and rivers, which, as their living environments, were naturally reflected in their poems. Since then, such lines are well known: "At sunset the river and islet turn cold. / The clouds of sorrow circle in the sky. / Only with short wings how to fly high? / But to wander in cold smoke and fog"[24] and "The great river running day and night, / My heart is filled with ceaseless grief. / Thinking that the capital is near, / I realise the path back is long".[25] It is hard to imagine that poets who have seen only a few mountains and rivers could have created abundant landscape poems. It is not only about diversity, but about universality. In "The water-separated green mountains are like home",[26] does it also show the love of homeland in the traveller's wandering experience? It can be expanded to the singing showing the love of the home country. All of these are in harmony with the poets' lives. Without life, the source of literature, there is no poetry. Moreover, landscape poetry, never a still life painting, can never be developed without life. Of course, the Southern Dynasties were still dominated by great families. At that time, the literary circle was not completely free from the monopoly of the gentry. Most of the writers were from the middle and upper classes, and they were still not rich. Therefore, their achievements on landscape poetry could not be remarkably high, except for those of Xie Lingyun, Xie Tiao, Yin Keng, and He Xun, who are generally recognised in history. However, the life of a travelling official is different from a decadent life, and a traveller's theme is not divorced from reality, taking which as the general

24 Bao Zhao. "Farewell to Captain Fu".
25 Xie Tiao. "To my Fellow Officials at Western Office in my Temporary Envoy to the Secondary Capital before Leaving New Forest at Night for the Capital".
26 Dai Shulun. "On the Landscape of Zhichuan".

How did landscape poetry come into being? 65

living content of the writers at that time, landscape poetry came into being, but only reached an ordinary level.

It is in the Tang Dynasty that poets really improved and developed landscape poetry. This is also inseparable from the overall development of economy, politics, and culture in the Tang Dynasty. Then, simpler landscape poems appeared more frequently, including short ones such as "Song of the Hengjiang River", "Looking at the Falls at Mount Lu", "Miscellaneous Poems at Huangfu Yue's Cloud Stream"; middle ones such as "The Hanjiang River View", "The Zhongnan Mountains", "Admiring Mount Tai"; long ones such as "Dragon Gate Pavilion", "Cypress Ferry"; and much longer ones like "Hard are the Trails of Shu".[27] At the same time, this shows that simple landscape poems did not appear before works combining landscape and living experience; on the contrary, they appeared to fulfil the growing requirement of expressing lives. The landscape was initially used as the foreshadowing of the poetic content, then widely combined with it, and finally some poems purely on landscape and sceneries appeared among a large number of works. Even though these landscape poems do not directly tell the specific content of life on the surface, in fact, the flavour of life, the background of thoughts, and the spirit of the time are clearly visible. From Cao Cao's "Watching the Vast Sea" on, simple landscape poetry is not just a simple description of scenery. Li Bai notes that "The monastery clouds are full of monk spirit. / How can such a scenery satisfy people's hearts?"[28] This outstanding poet in landscape poetry "Enjoying visiting famous mountains all my lifetime" also feels that the landscape he usually loves has become a dull image when he feels extremely depressed. It is in life that landscape poetry grows, develops, and flourishes.

The landscape and scenery might be the content of landscape poetry; however, they are more closely related to a general national form. From "The crescent moon shining over the Nine States" to "The crescent moon over the beautiful city of Tando", and from "Half a moon climbs up" to "Singing of the stars and the moon", until the singing of all natural sceneries including the "clear water and blue sky", all these cultivated forms of expression enjoyed by different ethnic groups are based on landscape poetry as well as on life. Marx states in the preface to *A Contribution to the Critique of Political Economy* that "an objet d'art creates a public that has an artistic taste and is able to enjoy beauty—and the same can be said of any other product". If Chinese landscape poetry has ever played such a role in Chinese nationality, then in the process of dialectical development, it should be developed and continue to be loved by people.

---

27 Li Bai. "Six Songs of the Hengjiang River", "Looking at the Falls at Mount Lu", and "Hard are the Trails of Shu"; Wang Wei. "Miscellaneous Poems at Huangfu Yue's Cloud Stream", "The Hanjiang River View", and "The Zhongnan Mountains"; Du Fu. "Admiring Mount Tai", "Dragon Gate Pavilion", and "Cypress Ferry".

28 Li Bai. "At Jiangxia To Wei Bing, the County Head of Nanling".

66 *How did landscape poetry come into being?*

The original source of landscape poetry is the foreshadowing of landscape in folk songs, which means that it is always closely linked with life, because the foreshadowing of landscape originally appears to bring imagination into life. However, just as foreshadowing can often be used in many lyrics, some landscape poems can often arouse a variety of associations. "Lush mulberries grow on the mountain; / Beautiful lotus flowers in the pond" may not necessarily be followed by "I did not see Zidu my love, / But saw you such a bad boy" as in *Shijing*. It is difficult to exactly tell the theme of "The spring water is full in the four rivers; / The summer clouds fly over rare peaks; / The autumn moon shines bright light; / The winter ridge shows a lonely pine",[29] but it can produce a wide range of foreshadowing effect. It's also the case in Li Bai's "Thoughts on a Cold Night while Drinking Alone: An Answer to Wang the 12th" with a strong thought, which begins with:

> Last night a snow fell in Wuzhong,
> Making you happy as Ziyou.
> Floating clouds of thousands of *li* surround green hills.
> The lonely moon is swimming in the bluish sky.
> The moon is alone and cold, the River of Stars clear,
> The Big Dipper scattered with the bright Hesperus.
> You miss me for the wine drinking on a frosty night
> By the golden well with ice on the jade balustrade.
> A hundred years of life is a flickering moment;
> Let's drink heartily for the eternal emotions.

The images and sceneries here also seem to be acceptable if used as the opening lines of some of Li Bai's other poems. As for the first four lines of Meng Haoran's "Passing by My Old Friend's Farmstead": "My old friend prepared chicken rice, / And invited me to his farmstead. / Green trees are surrounding the village, / While verdant hills lie far from the town". They became a separate poem circulated independently with the original poem of eight lines. This means that the artistic images have their relative independence, which of course means that they are not absolutely independent. If we think the images are unconscious, pointless, and content-free because there is no specific language to explain the ideas in some landscape poems, then how can we understand the artistic creations like music that have no specific language at all? Or will they all become riddles? Moreover, although landscape poetry originated from foreshadowing, it did not stop at that. As mentioned earlier, pure landscape poetry is still a minority. What it is in poetry is what light music is in music. Its role in poetry should be neither

---

29 This poem is entitled "Four Seasons" in the *Collection of Tao Yuanming*. However, Tang Han's *Poetry Annotations of Jingjie* states that it is the "Poetry of Seasonal Spirits" by Gu Kaizhi.

overrated nor underestimated. Without the development and achievements of these landscape poems, the richness and variety of classical Chinese poetry would have inevitably been reduced.

Landscape poems do not stop at foreshadowing, so they are often enlightening. At the same time, the quatrains from folk songs have one of the most enlightening forms in a variety of poetry styles. Thus, the two can be combined, as in Zu Yong's "Looking at the Remaining Snow at the Zhongnan Mountains", in which there are only four lines "The shadowy ridges of Zhongnan are pretty / For the white snows like floating in the clouds. / The forest top is shining with the setting sun; / The city of Chang'an becomes colder at dusk". However, the enlightenment was intentionally retained in the quatrain.[30] Other landscape quatrains such as "A Quatrain", "Looking at the Sky-Gate Mount", "Leaving the White Emperor City Early", "Ascending the Stork Tower", and "Song of Liangzhou"[31] that have been sung endlessly are widely loved by people for their rich enlightenment, though somewhat tendentious. However, the singing of "landscape poetry" and "quatrains" precisely shows their relationships with folk songs.

The capture of images often leads to excessive exaggeration of artistic skills, which is a common practice; new artistry, therefore, often open a convenient door to formalism. *Chuci* creatively developed the richness of poetic language after *Shijing*, but opened a convenient door for the parallelism of Han *fu*. The new development and achievements of landscape poetry also brought about the poetic style of "cherishing not the flowery"; however, these cannot be attributed to *Chuci* or landscape poetry. The final determinant is still the time and the writers' lived experiences.

The epoch-making appearance of landscape poetry did not occur in the darkest and most chaotic time of the Southern Dynasties. On the contrary, it appeared at a time when the situation was improving, and the political and economic development in the Southern Dynasties were more enlightened and prosperous. Isn't it another fact?

This research only aims to explain that the appearance of landscape poetry is not based on ideas far from reality, nor on gardens, fields, or seclusion lives, but on a natural product at a more mature stage of the feudal economic development that goes beyond *Shijing* and *Chuci* in the progressive understanding of natural beauty. If we can clarify it first, it might benefit further studies on the landscape poetry in the Tang Dynasty.

April 1961

Originally published in *Literary Review*, 1961 (3)

---

30 *Records of the Tang Poetry* notes: "In an imperial test of 'Looking at the Remaining Snow at the Zhongnan Mountains,' Zu Yong just wrote four lines and handed in. When asked why, Yong said: 'The meaning ends'".

31 Du Fu. "Four Quatrains" No. 3; Li Bai. "Looking at the Sky-Gate Mount" and "Leaving the White Emperor City Early"; Wang Zhihuan. "Ascending the Stork Tower" and "Song of Liangzhou".

5 Language of the Tang poetry

The great achievements of poetry in the Tang Dynasty have drawn extensive attention from scholars of the past dynasties as they hope to draw something new from it for reference. Before the Tang poetry, the Jian'an era provided a good example of poetry writing. However, the Tang Dynasty becomes a much better example because of the Tang poetry. Even though the examples are only to be referenced, not imitated, the Tang poetry provides a really good example. It follows the poetry writing style of the Jian'an era, but it is different from and far superior to the latter. There are many reasons for the widespread reputation of the Tang poetry in the reader's mind. However, its achievement in language is undoubtedly one of the important reasons. Poetry is more "an art of language" in its true sense, compared with all the other literary forms. For instance, we can perform a pantomime without language, but poetry without language is unthinkable. Certainly, poetry can be found in painting, but it is another kind of art. Poetry has a high demand for language. The discrepancy of a single Chinese character in diction often determines the artistic conception of a poem, which highlights the special importance of language in poetry. In fact, the general impression left by the Tang poetry is that it is more easily understood and felt than not only the poetry preceding it, but also that following it in the Song, Yuan, Ming, and Qing Dynasties. Therefore, it is worth our sustained attention.

Many writers in history have noticed this characteristic, but their understanding is too simple. They believe that as long as the language is easy to understand, the poetry will be easy to comprehend. But unfortunately, they have underestimated the richness and vividness of language. The linguistic characteristic of the Tang poetry is not merely manifested in its simplicity, but in its "profundity in simplicity". What is the relationship between profundity and simplicity? Actually, the simplicity is based on and is interwoven with profundity. Therefore, it is simple but rich in meaning, easy but profound in thinking. The richness and profundity are essential to the mastery of the art. There have been, historically, such works presenting appealing images but weak generality in thinking, like some poems with strong artistic sensibility but written in difficult and obscure language. They might have strong or weak thoughts, but their language is usually obscure, as shown in certain works by Li He (also Li Ho, 790–816). This is what is called profundity without simplicity.

Poetry is the art of language, and the main characteristic of art is its images. Whether the language of poetry can go deep into the realm of images, in fact, is related to whether the poetry can fully occupy its realm of art. However, language, based on concepts, first requires a high degree of unity in profundity and simplicity. To adapt to this requirement, the language of poetry has established its own special form: a language rich in flexibility and melody, in which unbridled imagination and sober rationality, intuitive perception, and explicit concepts are dialectically intertwined; a language as if stereoscopic, meanwhile simple and profound, rather than explicit and straightforward. It is this internal demand that leads to the external language form of completeness, unity, and rhythm. The rhythmic form of poetry is not an ornament, nor is it merely for a simple purpose of easy recitation. A simple emphasis on this purpose will be of little help in answering the following question: "Why do not the lines in a play need to be recited easily?" Thus, to acquire the essence of the language of poetry, we must gradually explore poetry writing in practice and gradually make it mature in this regard. The essence is born out of constant and intensive improvement on the basis of the common language. This requires years of time.

When the language of poetry on the basis of classical Chinese has reached the most mature stage, and when the real life in China's feudal society has reached the healthiest stage on the basis of its cultural and economic development, the Tang poetry appeared on this historic peak. After that, the feudal society went downhill, which inevitably affected the development of poetry. As for the language itself, the so-called *gubaihua* (ancient written vernacular Chinese) had more presence after the Tang Dynasty, showing that classical Chinese gradually moved away from the language of life; thus the language of poetry formed on the basis of classical Chinese becomes fossilised and aged after the peak of maturity. The Tang poetry just appeared in the best time of social development as well as of poetic language development in ancient history. The Tang Dynasty is an incredibly prosperous period for poetry writing. It is beyond the past and beyond the following dynasties; thus, it is of great significance for us today to review the historical facts in this period.

I The poeticisation of the language of poetry

Though the Tang Dynasty is its golden age, five-character and seven-character poetry become mature after a long process.[1] This is what I mean by poeticisation. First, five-character and seven-character lines are extracted

---

1 Five-character poetry is one of the ancient Chinese poetic forms. It is composed of four or eight or more lines. In each line there are five Chinese characters. Similarly, seven-character poetry has seven Chinese characters in each line.

70　*Language of the Tang poetry*

from the everyday prose, but they are not entirely the same. They are more poetic not only in form but in grammar and vocabulary. In fact, they have appeared sporadically even in the era of *Shijing*, in which four-character poetry has reached its peak. A good example is a stanza in the "Dew on the Path" in *South of Shao*.

谁谓雀无角, 何以穿我屋; 谁谓女无家, 何以速我狱。虽速我狱, 室家不足。[shuíwèi què wújiǎo, héyǐ chuān wǒwū; shuíwèi nǚ wújiā, héyǐ sù wǒyù. suīsù wǒyù, shìjiā búzú.] (Who says sparrows are hornless? / Why peck at my house? / Who says you are homeless, / Why threaten me with prison? / You threaten with prison; / Your home is worthless.)[2]

Another example is in "The 30th Year of Duke Xiang" in the *Commentary of Zuo*:[3]

舆人诵之曰: "取我衣冠而褚之, 取我田畴而伍之, 孰杀子产? 吾其与之。" [yúrén sòngzhī yuē: "qǔwǒ yīguàn ér chǔzhī, qǔwǒ tiánchóu ér wǔzhī, shúshā zǐchǎn? wúqí yuzhī.] (Many people chant about it: "Take my dress and store up it, / Measure all my land and levy taxes. / Who will kill Zichan? / I will help him".)[4]

In "Tangong (part II)" in *The Book of Rites*:

成人曰: "蚕则绩而蟹有匡, 范则冠而蝉有緌, 兄则死而子皋为之衰。" [chéngrén yuē: "cánzéjì ér xièyǒukuāng, fànzéguàn ér chányǒuruí, xiōngzésǐ ér zǐgāo wéizhī shuāi"] (Cheng people say: "silkworms have silk and crabs have crusts; / Bees have heads and cicadas have mouths; / With his brother dead, / Zigao wears sable for him".)[5]

There are other seven-character lines like "彼其之子美如英[bǐqí zhīzǐ měirúyīng] (That man is handsome as a blossom)"[6] and "交交黄鸟止于棘 [jiāojiāo huángniǎo zhǐyújí] (Chirping yellow birds rest in the jujube)".[7] However, these occasional five-character or seven-character lines are composed spontaneously rather than intentionally; they are only exceptions to four-character lines, without arousing much attention among people or serving as models for them. Only when five-character and seven-character

---

2　In the original Chinese, the first four clauses are five-character lines and the last two four-character lines. All translations of the Chinese characters in this chapter are literal.
3　Also *Chronicle of Zuo*, or *Zuozhuan*.
4　In the original Chinese, the first two clauses in the quotation are seven-character lines.
5　ibid.
6　"At a Low and Damp Bank of the Fen River" in *The Air of Wei*.
7　"Yellow Birds" in *The Air of Qin*.

Language of the Tang poetry 71

lines are recognised as typical poetic forms, was this phenomenon possibly noticed later?

In the poetry circle, the intentional breach of the "four-character" norm begins with *Chuci*. To achieve this goal, poets must create a poetic language from the daily language of prose. This is a new creative process bringing about highly poetic language, which usually symbolises the general maturity of the poetry circle. But *Chuci* does not represent a mature poetry circle. Although there is a great, mature poet like Qu Yuan, there is almost no other truly mature poet among the authors of *Chuci*, so *Chuci* and Qu Yuan have become almost synonymous. To the poetry circle, *Chuci* is just a strange forerunner of the more mature five-character and seven-character poetry circle because it has only collected 17 works by a few writers. It is neither so popular as the four-character poetry circle prevalent in the 15 states and in different styles of *feng*, *ya*, and *song*,[8] nor is it so popular as the five-character and seven-character poetry circle dominating the spectacular poetry world in the following 1,000 or 2,000 years. Therefore, *Chuci* is actually a bridge between the four- and five- or seven-character lines. It has no unified and universal form of its own. On the one hand, it breaks away from the former four-character lines; on the other, it encourages the future development of five-character or seven-character lines. Thus, *Chuci* has experienced both a prosaic process and a poeticisation. The prosaic process aims to break away from the old four-character poetry, and to make it closer to the common language of life, while the poetic process is to establish a unified, universally significant poetic form based on the new language.

As mentioned above, *Chuci*, developed at the peak of the pre-Qin prose works, [9] has undergone both prosaic and poetic processes. On the one hand, its language becomes more and more vivid, with the art of antithesis; on the other, a new form is used throughout poems like "Ode to the Fallen Country" and "Mountain Spirits". The nature of the lines is that the "three-character end" takes the place of the "two-character end" of four-character poetry. This nature of the "three-character rhythm" has a direct influence on the initial formation of seven-character poetry in the Han Dynasty. As for the relationship between *Chuci* and seven-character poetry, there are two clues on the surface. The first is to double the lines in *Shijing*, and omit the last character, as shown in "后皇嘉树橘来服(兮)[hòuhuáng jiāshù júláifú (xī)] (Virtuous trees on earth, oranges adapt not (Oh))" from "Ode to the Orange", in which the last Chinese character "兮[xī] (a carrier sound)" is omitted to make it a seven-character line. More obvious seven-character lines can be found in "Questions to Heaven", including "遂古之初谁传道(之), 上下未形何由考(之) [suígǔ zhīchū shuíchuándào (zhī), shàngxià wèixíng héyóukǎo (zhī)]

8 The terms *feng*, *ya*, and *song*, respectively, refer to the airs of states, court hymns, and eulogies.
9 Lin Geng. "On 'Crossing the River' from the Punctuation of *Chuci*", "The Origin of 'Nine Songs' is not Ernan Folk Song", etc.

72 Language of the Tang poetry

(From the very beginning, who passes on (it), / No Heaven and Earth, how to explore (it))", in which the last character "之[zhī] (it)" is omitted, and "师望在肆昌何识, 鼓刀扬声后何喜[shīwàng zàisì chānghéshí, gǔdāo yángshēng hòuhéxǐ] (Jiang in the butcher's, Zhou recognises not. Jiang comes to fame, glad Zhou becomes)", etc., in which there are just seven characters in each part. The second clue is concerned with the whole new form of "×××兮×××", based on the poeticisation after the prosaic process. Such seven-character poetry initially appears in the combination of "three, three, seven characters", in which the first and second lines are three-character, and the third line is seven-character. It reflects the nature of the "three-character rhythm" created in *Chuci*; at the same time, the carrier sound "兮" in the middle can be omitted or turned into a content word, which still exists in today's *Kuaiban*.[10] Most of the occasional seven-character proverbs in the pre-Qin Dynasty and the Two Han Dynasties belong to the former, while the early seven-character poetry in the *yuefu* ballads in the Han Dynasty belongs to the latter, such as "An Elegy: Dew on the Plant Xie", "Haoli the Dwelling Place of Souls", and "East of the Pingling Tomb" in *Melodious Ballads*, and "Fighting in the City South", "Your Steed is Golden", and "Emperor Wu Comes to the Huizhong Palace" in *Army Songs*. A large number of seven-character lines, which predominate over the five-character lines in the *yuefu* ballads in the Western Han Dynasty (202 BCE–8CE), are replaced by five-character lines in the Eastern Han Dynasty. This prominent phenomenon vividly demonstrates that the early seven-character poetry is directly derived from *Chuci*, and that five-character poetry is the combination of the three-character rhythm of *Chuci* and the two-character rhythm of *Shijing*. Based on the original tradition and line length of *Shijing*, five-character lines are more likely to be accepted, compared with seven-character lines. However, the "three-character end" as its basic rhythm pattern, similar to seven-character lines, is also a result of the poeticisation of *Chuci*. Lines consisting of a five-character line and a seven-character line like "蒿里谁家地? 聚敛魂魄无贤愚 [hāolǐ shuíjiādì? jùliǎn húnpò wúxiányú] (Haoli is in whose territory? / Gathered are all spirits, clever or stupid)" show that five-character and seven-character lines are homologous from the beginning, so that they can coexist for a long time and become the basic form for the prosperity of the Tang poetry.

In fact, the poeticisation does not reach its peak with the maturity of five-character lines, which has brought forth the peak of the Jian'an era. However, a higher peak is not reached until seven-character poetry becomes mature in the golden age of the Tang poetry. They are about 400 years apart. During this period, the poeticisation of five-character poetry, in its mature form, is concentrated in images. It had been sweeping through the literary circles for about 400 years in the Six Dynasties, which include the Wei and Jin

---

10 *Kuaiban*, a form of oral storytelling performance, is popular in northern China and somewhat similar to rapping in English.

Dynasties.[11] At that time, both prose and *fu*[12] gradually become similar to poetry in the poeticisation. From "*Fu* on Mounting a Building" by Wang Can (177–217) to "*Fu* of Sorrow to Jiangnan" by Yu Xin, almost all the content and language of the *fu* were developing around poetry as the centre, while "*Fu* on the Spring" by Yu Xin is mainly a seven-character chanting poem. But the more prominent is the poeticisation of prose. The prosperity of *pianwen* in the Six Dynasties is unprecedented in the history of Chinese literature, but in the Tang Dynasty when the poeticisation becomes mature with hundreds of flowers of poetry in full bloom, the *fu* and *pianwen* are nearing its close. This is, of course, related to the writers' class and lives in the Six Dynasties. However, in the Tang Dynasty the *fu* and *pianwen* are not entirely absent, but lacking are fresh creative works such as "*Fu* on Mounting a Building", "*Fu* of Sorrow to Jiangnan", and "Persuasion at Beishan Mountain". Neither does this era lack works with alternate lines, characteristic of prose and *pianwen* like *The Commentary on the Water Classic*, *On the Buddhist Temples in Luoyang*, etc. In the Song Dynasty, not only is the original prose restored, but *fu* becomes similar to prose. The contrast of the chronical development of different forms proves that the predominance of *pianwen* in the Six Dynasties is mainly a great wave around the rapid development of the poetic language, ebbing after the completion of poeticisation. As for the Tang poetry itself, of course, it further enriched the realm of poetic language on the basis of its maturity. In fact, there is a dialectic development of negation of the negation—it comes from everyday language and goes back to everyday language. If the Six Dynasties are at the stage of deliberate poetic pursuit, then the Tang poetry has reached the peak of rule-based writing that is nevertheless following the poet's own inclinations, which certainly belongs to a higher stage, having gone beyond the intentional poetic pursuit. It is precisely because of the poetic pursuit since the Jian'an era, and the need to extract the language of poetry from the language of prose that leads to the poeticisation tendency of prose itself. This tendency has laid a more extensive foundation, and its end is the true maturity of the language of poetry, which does not refer to a specific writer or a certain work, but the general language level at a time. At this level, as long as the author has authentic content, he can fully represent it in his writing. The overall achievement of the Tang poets depends first on the content and spirit of the era, which will be discussed elsewhere. However, if the language level of the time is not high enough, it would be difficult to achieve the prosperity of poetry. Not all good content will naturally become a good poem, nor will everyone be an outstanding poet, nor will a profound thought

---

11 The Six Dynasties is a collective term for six Chinese dynasties in China during the periods of the Three Kingdoms (220–280) consisting of Wei (220–266), Shu (221–263), Wu (222–280), Jin (265–420), and Northern (386–581) and Southern (420–589) Dynasties. It also coincides with the period of the Sixteen Kingdoms (304–439).

12 *Fu*, variously translated as rhapsody or poetic exposition, is a form of Chinese rhymed prose dominant in the Han Dynasties (206 BCE–220CE).

74 *Language of the Tang poetry*

inevitably bring about excellent art. Of course, the relationship between them is close; thus, we should pay great attention to the decisive role the thought and content of life play, and fully understand how important language is to poetry, a typical language art.

The poeticisation of language, to be specific, is the formation of its own special language on the basis of ordinary language, which is prominently reflected in such "function words"[13] indispensable in prose writing as "之[zhī]", "乎[hū]", "者[zhě]", "也[yě]", "矣[yǐ]", "焉[yān]", and "哉[zāi]". They can be omitted in five-character poetry in the Qi and Liang Dynasties. This is by no means easily achieved. As long as we think about today's *baihuashi* (written vernacular poetry), if we all should omit the character "的[de]", which is equivalent to the aforementioned "之", we will find it difficult and unnatural. This is purely a question on the language of poetry, a matter which is never raised in the genre of prose. However, whether some characters can be omitted or not is a measurement of the refinement and flexibility of the language of poetry. The "function words" in prose are more than those mentioned above, and what can be omitted in a poem is not merely "function words", as can be seen in such common poetic structures as "妖童宝马铁连钱, 娼妇盘龙金屈膝[yāotóng bǎomǎ tiěliánqián, chāngfù pánlóng jīnqūxī] (Frivolous child precious horse iron joint coins, / street girls coiled dragon gold screen hinges)", in which no verb is used at all. The grammar in famous lines like "一洗万古凡马空[yīxǐ wàngǔ fánmǎkōng]" (One wash ten thousand years ordinary horses empty) can only exist in poetry. In fact, the considerable reduction of some usually necessary words in poetry will not make people feel inconvenienced or uneasy. On the contrary, the language becomes more focused, more flexible, and more typical. This is a high-level refinement as well as a sign of the poetic development of language.

Whether this sign exists or not makes a difference. In the Tang poetry, although the achievement of *Gutishi* (ancient poetry) is probably higher than that of *Jintishi* (modern poetry), the sign indicates the general level of language in the poetry circle. Whether this level is high enough makes a difference too. In *Implied Criticism of Poetry*, Ge Lifang (?–1164) states that "probably the seemingly plain expressions should come from the flowery ones; removing the flowery expressions can create a plain artistic conception. If so, Tao Qian and Xie Lingyun cannot be surpassed".[14] Thus, Su Dongpo (also Su Shi, 1037–1101) thinks that the poetry of Tao Yuanming is "apparently plain but actually flowery, seemingly barren but factually fertile";[15] "at first glance, it seems careless and thoughtless, but after second thought awesome expressions are found".[16] Huang Tingjian (1045–1105) also thinks that

---

13 Function words in Chinese include adverbs, prepositions, conjunctions, auxiliary words, interjections, and onomatopoeia.
14 Tao Qian and Xie Lingyun (385–433) are famous for their plain artistic conception in plain words.
15 Su Shi. "A Letter to Su Zhe".
16 Huihong. "Evening Talk at the Cold Studio".

Language of the Tang poetry   75

"Tao Yuanming is a genuine writer, not constrained by rules. Even so, those apt at skills doubt that he is too clumsy".[17] It is obvious that a work that seems plain and simple might not be really plain or simple. Each poem has its own merits. Certainly, it does not mean that the language level in *Gutishi* was not very high before the appearance of *Jintishi*. As mentioned before, it only indicates the general level of the poetic language of the era, which is only a basic condition, while a truly outstanding poet will always rise above the general level, and the high prosperity of the poetry circle is based on this general level. One of the reasons why the Tang poetry is not easy to surpass is the development and maturity of its language of poetry. It would be unthinkable that the Tang poets, though talented, could fully exert their ability without the high language level of the era, as is the case with the poets in other times. In other words, how can we say that the poets in other times are not so talented?

The poeticisation of the language of poetry is concerned with not only the refinement and flexibility of language, but the richness of images. To capture the images and to activate the poet's thinking in images, the most extensive world of resources is the natural scenery, which is the objectification of Nature. From Cao Cao's "Watching the Vast Sea", poetry began to intensively express a wealth of thoughts and feelings through the scenery in Nature. From the time of *Shijing* on, the natural scenery has been an element of the writing technique of foreshadowing, which is used to introduce the subject by mentioning other things first. It began to enter all realms of poetry then. This deepened the vividness and richness of language, and gradually promoted the further development of landscape poetry. Of course, the vividness of poetic language does not rely entirely on natural scenery, but the flourishing of landscape poetry undoubtedly encouraged its development, and became the new sign of the language of images. Before the Sui and Tang Dynasties, such compositions became familiar and could be handled with great efficiency. The degree of skillfulness can be seen in allusions, which are used in poetry and prose to briefly summarise, to narrate anecdotes of the past in referring to the present, or to express complex meanings through simple allusions, like "Zhong Yi, prisoned, plays the music of Chu; / Zhuang Xi, famed, in the Yue dialect, would moan".[18]

The images in allusions mainly depend on the original characters in the story. If there is no story or vivid character in the allusion, then there is no image but boring materials. Since the development of landscape poetry, the images in allusions began not to rely entirely on the original story, but to

---

17 Huang Tingjian. "Written after Yike's Poem".
18 The whole poem reads: "Zhong Yi, secluded, plays the music of Chu, / Zhuang Xi, famed, in the Yue dialect, would moan. / Homesickness is the same for me and you. / How can we be unlike, blessed or unknown?" In Wang Can: "*Fu* on Mounting a Building". In this poem, there are two allusions. The first is to Zhong Yi, who was imprisoned in the Kingdom of Jin but often played the music of Chu where he was born. The second is to Zhuang Xi, who was a famous officer in the Chu state, but when he was ill, he would moan in the dialect of Yue where he was born.

76 *Language of the Tang poetry*

rely on all the objects in Nature directly taken from the living environment, which opens up a new realm in allusion. As a master of this skill, Yu Xin uses such allusions as "red sun", "flying magpie", "purple swallow", and "morning breeze". These allusions on the four steeds in "Shooting on Horseback in the Hualin Park" are merely used to praise the precious steeds. It should be easy, but the new combination has created a complex image that the four steeds are distinctively running in the morning breeze towards the morning sun. Similar expressions include "A phoenix falls in the morning sun, / In the wild a *qilin* (Chinese unicorn) is injured".[19] It visualises the old allusion of no image, and makes it very fresh and vivid. Another example is:

> The tortoise says this place is cold,
> The crane wonders at the snow this year.[20]

Certain allusions have been used in such a wintery scene, but in the above lines, the implied association between the ice cracks and the cracks on tortoise shells, along with the flying snow with the feathers of cranes, deepens the reader's understanding of the world of ice and snow. It works very well in allusions. Moreover, when there is no allusion, ingenious expressions would be within easy reach. For instance:

> The frost becomes white with white willows,
> The moon goes round the round tomb.[21]

The white of the frost is similar to the white of the willow, and the roundness of the moon is similar to the roundness of the tomb. Similar things stimulate similar feelings and lead to heart-felt leaps of the imagination. Consider another example:

> One inch, two inches of fish,
> Three poles, two poles of bamboo.[22]

It is so easy, but it is so natural. In "The snow is three feet thick, / The ice is one fathom cold",[23] and "A clump of fragrant grass makes people stay; / A few feet of silk floats across the way",[24] the numbers of little importance also play a distinctive role. However, this easiness comes from hardships,

---

19 Yu Xin. "An Inscription on Thinking of the Past". Here *qilin* or kirin refers to a mythical hooved chimerical creature known in Chinese and other East Asian cultures, and myth has it that it appears with the imminent arrival or passing of a sage or an illustrious ruler.
20 Yu Xin. "On a Little Garden".
21 Yu Xin. "Epitaph of Houmochen Daosheng".
22 Yu Xin. "*Fu* on a Little Garden".
23 Yu Xin. "Visiting the Public Prosecution Office on the Lunar New Year's Day".
24 Yu Xin. "*Fu* On the Spring".

Language of the Tang poetry 77

just like an excellent high jumper—how easy he makes it look when he flies over the pole. This effortlessness is actually the result of long, hard practice, without which the facility would never come. And the higher the jump, the higher the accuracy of the gesture, the easier it seems; this creates an illusion that the highest art seems natural and effortless. As a master carpenter will not show off his skills in playing with an axe, we praise the masterpieces that do not betray traces of the intentional skills behind them. However, we seldom think about how to achieve that. Of course, there are nearly "natural works as if from heaven" in poetry, which are considered only occasional and impossible to create with skills.

Basically, things happen in randomness and coincidence, but if we only rely on them and fail to grasp the real necessity, the "natural works as if from heaven" would be elusive. If so, will not the prosperity of the Tang poetry be like waiting for a hare to hit the trunk and kill itself?[25] In fact, even the "natural works as if from heaven" in folk ballads are not mature until they are thoroughly and constantly polished over generations. Of course, in the Six Dynasties, the traces of skills still existed, even in Yu Xin's later works. For instance:

The dewdrops cry and fall like a string of beads;
The fireflies are shattered like a stream of sparkles.[26]

It is a unique expression, but it cannot be said to be a work by "a master carpenter playing with an axe", which naturally requires a more in-depth unity of living activities and art. As for the language of art, its difficult poeticisation takes more than a short while. We do not appreciate works showing too many traces of skills, nor do we favour the sheer artistic pursuit more than ideological representation. Thus, it is unnecessary to repeat the process of "cherishing not the flowery" in the Six Dynasties. We can only be critical in accepting the ancients' experience, let alone the fact that ideas and thoughts can only benefit art rather than do harm to it, as shown in Yu Xin's later works. As for art, it is not a terrible thing. Even Du Fu has to "learn from Yin and He by heart",[27] and that does no harm to Du Fu's greatness with respect to his thoughts. The maturity of poetic language which might be very subjective is objectively achieved through long-term accumulation and painstaking writing practice and exploration. The development of poetic language from the Jian'an era to the Sui Dynasty paved the way for the Tang

---

25 A peasant in the state of Song (1114–286 BCE) once saw a fast-running hare hit a trunk, break its neck, and kill itself in his field. Then the peasant put down his hoe and waited by the trunk for another hare to turn up, but no more hares appeared. Thus, he became the laughing-stock of the state.

26 Yu Xin. "Imitation of a Song of Feelings".

27 Yin refers to Yin Keng (c. 511–c. 563), while He is the surname of He Xun (472–519). Both are famous for their polish of verses.

78   *Language of the Tang poetry*

poetry, as the steepest Three Gorges helps the Yangtze River vigorously rush down a thousand *li*. Because of the four prominent poets in the Early Tang,[28] the Tang poetry has entered the initial stage of brilliance based on the maturity of poetic language, as shown in Yang Jiong's "Piebald Horses":

> Royal roads, as flat as water, are arrayed;
> The official paths are string-straight and fast.
> The cart's shaft is adorned with nighttime's jade;
> The autumn wind into horsewhips is cast.

"The cart's shaft is made up by the night jade" has the remaining traces of the Six Dynasties, while "the autumn wind into horsewhips is cast" is not the language of that time (the "autumn wind" is also written as the "autumn gold", which is inferior in the artistic conception, but it is not the language of the Six Dynasties either). The pinnacle of the poetic language is clearly shown in the lines below:

> No one would bring you this song full of sad longing.
> How I wish the spring breeze to Yanran would it bring!
> But you're far away at the end of the blue sky!
> My watery eyes of yearning
> Have become teardrops' spring.
> Don't trust my heart's broken?
> Return! The bright mirror will reveal my feeling.[29]

There is no need for more proof that the language of poetry has reached its peak. This simple but profound singing is certainly inseparable from real life in the Tang Dynasty. Above all, life determines its language; but how well this language can serve life is still a matter of language.

From the Jian'an era to the Tang Dynasty, the poeticisation of language has gone through about 400 years to reach its pinnacle. This is the result of the era, as well as the internal law of language development and the writers' practice. In our modern time, this process can certainly be greatly shortened. How long it takes to establish a mature language of poetry from the vernacular prose mainly depends on our own efforts, but the process is necessary. It is unrealistic for a general level of poetic language to be mature in a short time. Time flies! Beginning from the new poetry movement in the May Fourth Movement in 1919 based on *baihua* (written vernacular Chinese), poetry writing has witnessed the elapse of about half a century, but until the 1960s there is not a new poetry form that is common for people to grasp, and

28 The four prominent poets in the Early Tang are Wang Bo (c. 650–676), Yang Jiong (c. 650–c. 693), Lu Zhaolin (c. 664–c. 713), and Luo Binwang (c. 638–684).
29 Li Bai. "Always in Yearning" or "Mutual Longing" (trans. W. J. B. Fletcher).

Language of the Tang poetry 79

equivalent to the mature forms in classical Chinese like five-character and seven-character lines. However, the maturity of poetic forms is only a most apparent sign of the poeticisation of language.

II The language of life and the richness of language

The reunification of China in the Sui and Tang Dynasties and the exchanges of the southern and northern literary styles are the social conditions under which the language of the Tang poetry matures. First, it is reflected in the further maturity of the poetic form, that is, seven-character poetry has opened a new chapter. As stated earlier, the five-character form is between the four-character form and seven-character form. In the Six Dynasties, four-character lines are outdated in form, but they are still very much alive in poetry writing. Cao Cao has more prominent masterpieces in four-character lines, and Tao Yuanming's "Motionless Cloud" and "Changing Seasons", fresh and perfect, are also of four-character lines. Especially, *pianwen*, *fu*, and *ming* (inscription), mainly composed of four-character lines, are developing almost equally with five-character lines. But the situation is completely different when seven-character poetry becomes mature and wins its place in history. After that, there are almost no excellent poems totally composed of four-character lines, and the literary forms like *pianwen* begin to decline too. This shows that the language of poetry has completely entered a new phase. Four-character lines have completed their historical mission and gone away, while five- and seven-character lines complementing each other have been dominating the poetry circle since then. At the same time, the Tang poetry reached its peak.

In comparison with five-character lines, seven-character lines seem more popular and catchy regarding the rhythm because the first half of five-character lines has the rhythm of four-character lines that seems more elegant and dignified. The total freedom of seven-character lines from four-character lines reflects a further liberation of language, which is the true meaning of the development of poetic forms in terms of its regularity, unity, and rhythm. It becomes true freedom after the rules of writing are mastered. And these rules are based on the reality of everyday language. The new poeticisation of language beginning from *Chuci* has reached the peak of maturity. It is clear and smooth, which is a sign of its full development, and everything seems so fresh and lively. This maturity process naturally has social causes. The Six Dynasties are full of aristocratic atmosphere; thus, when we just look back into the Eastern Jin Dynasty, in which the representative families of power and influence are flourishing, we find that most of the metaphysical poetry handed down are elegant four-character lines. And we can imagine that seven-character lines closer to spoken language are hard to maintain at that time.

With the unrefined "The Roads are Hard: An Imitation", Bao Zhao, as a representative poet from the poor or underprivileged families, greatly

80 *Language of the Tang poetry*

promoted the development of seven-character poetry. However outstanding his achievement is, he does not win the reputation he deserves in the poetry circle. This situation does not completely change until the reunification in the Sui and Tang Dynasties, which has ended the system of gentry clans. After the Eastern Jin Dynasty, the aristocratic power is gradually weakened. After Bao Zhao, seven-character poetry actually develops bit by bit, especially in the folk ballads of the Northern Dynasties, which are far better than those in the Southern Dynasties. These facts in the history of literature familiar to most Chinese readers will not be detailed here.

To explain why there have appeared so many seven-character lines in the northern folk ballads, we must recognise that the Northern Dynasties had not started sinicisation and frequent use of Chinese until the Northern Wei Dynasty (386–534). Thus, its system, culture, and language were at the initial stage. With great capacity for absorption and flexibility, the Northern Wei promoted the rapid development of everything. At the same time, the pure and forthright personality developed in nomadic life also affected the style of language. Seven-character lines, in essence, are not only simpler and more thorough lines of the "three-character rhythm", which can be easily found in the "three, three, seven characters" structure, but more unrefined and bold than five-character lines, making them more likely to appear in the North. At this time, the language of poetry in the Southern Dynasties has almost become mature. The northern songs pushed it to its peak with the fresh vitality from the language of life as if it were a catalyst. At the peak of this exchange between the northern and southern literary styles, seven-character poetry, like a trendsetter in the poetry circle, became the favoured one. A good case in point is "Pounding Clothes" by Wen Zisheng (495–547) from the Northern Dynasties: "Seeing the migrant wild geese from the Wasp Pass far, / Women in their boudoir set eyes on the Wolf Star". [30] This is one of the first communications between the northern and southern literary styles, and the author is considered "really like a Tang poet". Poets in the Southern Dynasties began from the seven-character "Song of the Northern Frontier", and laid a foundation for frontier fortress poetry in the Tang Dynasty as they are "wonderful in depicting the circumstances around the fortresses and passes". The language of poetry is then really "simple and profound", as shown in such lines as "a new moon hangs at the top of the city wall",[31] "The Big Dipper of seven stars crosses the midnight",[32] "Beholding, but not

---

30 The Wasp Pass refers to the Juyong Pass of the Great Wall in the North, while the boudoir, named after the couple bird *Yuanyang*, denotes the residence of women in the South. The Wolf Star is the binary star in the constellation Canis Major, also called Sirius or the Dog Star in English. The two lines state that coming across the migratory wild geese from the North, the women in the boudoir in the South looked at the Wolf Star and began missing their husbands fighting on the Northern frontier.

31 Cen Sen. "A Meeting with Judges at Liangzhou at Night".

32 Shen Quanqi. "Ancient Song".

Language of the Tang poetry 81

knowing, before the building",[33] and "Once noble or once humble, it tells of the true friendship".[34] Such language is close to the common language but so vivid, which is the most admirable in the language of the Tang poetry.

The language of the Tang poetry is both highly poetic and commonplace. The deeper foundation of this language is the Tang people's real life. China was reunited from division in the Tang Dynasty, and the Tang Empire reached the peak of the ancient feudal societies after getting rid of the remaining aristocratic power in the Six Dynasties. Its faith in life, great vision, and the Youth Spirit are shown in such lines as "The Sun is born on the sea just before the dawn. / The spring of Jiangnan walks into the year foregone",[35] and "No one knows who has cut out the leaves slim, / Winds of the second moon like scissors trim".[36] The rich and healthy breath of life, reflecting the life of the time, is close to poetry, as follows:

> Lower-Yangtze soldiers sometimes pass by Yangzhou,
> And play the flute before the ancient Lanling town.
> Going back by night fires to the out-town Fuchun,
> They hear storks cry in the Stone City in autumn wind.[37]
> The New Home wine worth ten thousand is so mellow,
> Enticing young roaming swordsmen in Xianyang town.
> They drink heartily to their spirit and renown,
> Leaving their steeds by a high inn to weeping willows.[38]

These pictures of life can only take place among the Tang people, and the language of poetry can only be produced in the Tang Dynasty. If the pre-Qin Dynasty is an era of contention of a hundred schools of thought, the Tang Dynasty is more so, with all flowers of thoughts blooming together. Music, dancing, painting, sculpture, and calligraphy are flourishing, inspiring life in different ways; this inevitably increases poets' sensitivity to new things and enriches their imagination of life. The language of the Tang poetry is only one of the most representative parts of the cultural life of the Tang Dynasty. It is of poetry and of life. It is different from a common language, only because it is more deeply rooted in images.

The poeticisation of language can be divided into two aspects, grammar and vocabulary, as is the case with language itself. In terms of grammar,

---

33 Lu Zhaolin. "The Antiquity of Chang'an".
34 Luo Binwang. "On the Imperial Capital".
35 Wang Wan. "Sojourning at the Beigu Hill".
36 He Zhizhang. "On Willows".
37 Wang Wei. "In the Same Rhyme Scheme as Cui Fu's Answer to his Younger Brother". "Fearing the winds' and storks' cry" is based on an allusion. When defeated by the Eastern Jin Army in the famous Feishui War in 383, the soldiers of the pre-Qin Dynasty were so feared that they thought the sound of the wind and the cry of the storks were signs of the pursuing enemy and fled away desperately.
38 Wang Wei. "Song of the Youth".

82 *Language of the Tang poetry*

the maturity of five-character or seven-character lines, the omission of "function words", the fresh styles, etc., make the writing more concise, more natural, and more liberated. As for the vocabulary, it is abundant. The vocabulary based on life is formed in the practice of poetry writing. When a poet writes a poem, very rarely is it the poet himself who creates the form, grammar, vocabulary, etc. It is based instead on the countless achievements of himself and his predecessors in the realm. An outstanding poet is different from those ordinary people in that he is better at absorbing the cumulative achievements and using them creatively. In this sense, a mature poem can be said to be both personal and collective. Moreover, the accumulation of vocabulary cannot be done overnight.

The vocabulary of poetry does not necessarily mean that there is another vocabulary besides the vocabulary culled from life. Such a vocabulary is occasional, close to allusions, but not identical to them. For example, "golden wave" is used as "moonlight", "silvery sea" as "snowy scenery", "lotus" as "feathered curtain", and "jade chopsticks" as "tears". They can be used in poetry writing if appropriate, but they cannot be totally relied on just as poetry writing does not mainly rely on allusions. The images in poetry best come directly from life. Thus, in the preface to *The Realm of Poetry*, it is stated that

> 'Missing you like the flowing water' is what we see, 'A high terrace has more sad winds' is what we feel, 'In early morning, I mount the Longshan mountain' contains no allusion, 'The bright moon is shining on the snow' is not from classics or history, and that most of the best expressions, ancient or modern, are not pieced together or borrowed, but directly created.

This at least shows the most common truth, on which the universal prosperity of poetry is based. However, how can words in everyday life become poetic words? This is still inseparable from the actual life.

From the Han Empire to the Tang Empire, the development of China's feudal society is tortuous and different in its maturation process, but all of them belong to the rising stage with the same basic life, which, in 500 years, has not dramatically changed but has matured and reached the peak of the feudal society. Months and years passing by, they have accumulated living experience and perceptions of life. Think about your hometown, in which you have lived for decades without a drastic change, but every piece of wood and every stone will remind you of rich feelings and mental images of life. For example:

> In the fortress of Han under the moon from Qin,
> No men back from a ten-thousand *li* march are seen.
> With the Dragon City's Flying Chief, we would win;
> No steeds of the Hu invaders could pass Mount Yin.[39]

39 Wang Changling. "Off the Fortress".

Language of the Tang poetry   83

The very words "fortress", "moon", and "mount", handed down from the Qin to the Han until the Tang Dynasty, have accumulated vast living history of the people. The depth and breadth of the feeling of life they can evoke are of universal significance! That's why the poem can be sung so vividly as a representative work. Only the three words—"fortress", "moon", and "mount"—linked together will produce quite vivid imagery, let alone the whole poem. Isn't it a common feeling in the Tang Dynasty? Let us look at the following example:

> The green willow boughs are hanging down to the ground.
> The willow flowers are flying around far and near,
> When the branches are plucked, the flowers disappear,
> Will people bidding farewell go back or linger round?[40]

The word "willow" is also so familiar in our life. However, poeticisation is not merely the process of being familiar with our life. Like the relationship between the superstructure and foundation, the formation of a nationality's psychology and character is determined by not only its life but its cultural tradition. From "When I left here, / Willows shed tears"[41] in *Shijing* to "Verdant grass grows along the river banks; / Green willows in the garden are flourishing" in "Nineteen Ancient Poems", the images of the "willow" just occasionally appeared in poetry at the beginning. However, the "willow" has already established a close relationship with "spring" and "wanderers", and gradually walked into our lives. According to the *Yellow Map of Three Districts*:

> The Baqiao Bridge is a bridge over water to the east of the Chang'an City. People in the Han Dynasty often see off their friends here and pluck willows to bid farewell.

Tao Yuanming calls himself Mister Five Willows. Wang Gong (?–398) is praised as "bright as a willow in the spring". And a large number of "willows" appear in poetry after the "Lyrics on Plucking Willows" in the Northern Dynasties. Then, after the reunification of China in the Sui and Tang Dynasties, the "willow", of poetry and of life, has become a most poetic image in life, following the life of wanderers and frontiersmen in an age of brilliance. To this day, we have proverbs like "In early spring, people watch willows along the river". If this can be regarded as a general national expression, we can learn more about these words. So long as we think of the "wine" or "sword" in ancient poems like "For compiling, candles are burnt short. / Gazing at swords, we drink wine long",[42] and then think of the corresponding

---

40 Anonymous [Sui Dynasty]. "Bidding Farewell".
41 "Minor Court Hymns: Picking Vetches".
42 Du Fu. "An Evening Banquet at Zuo's Manor".

84   *Language of the Tang poetry*

items we have today, we will find that none of them is so poetic in life. As a matter of fact, the tea has not taken the place of the wine; cigarettes have not become poetic—let alone the modern weapons, none of which can be compared with ancient swords. Similarly, the ancients' horses, equivalent to bikes or cars today, and the ancients' wide sleeves, equivalent to shopping bags today, have become vivid and poetic words in classical poetry. Poetic lines about the "rain" include "On the dark river the rain will come. / The early wind turns the waves white", "The night rain dripped on vacant steps. / The dawn darkened the light in the room", "When cold rain came to River Wu at night", "In days of little rain, the Luci Hill top is sunny", "In the Tomb-Sweeping days, the drizzle falls endlessly", "Misty rain falls on the neat river grass", etc.[43] The rain is just the ordinary rain, but in poetic language, it gradually becomes a deeply imaginative word, and its richness and universality is more prominent in the Tang Dynasty. For instance:

A morning rain has washed Weicheng so clean;
The inn looks thriving in fresh willows green.
My friend, raise a toast with wine! One more cup!
West of the Sunny Pass no friend cheers you up.[44]

Just like the aforementioned "pass", "mountain", and "moon", the images "rain", "willow", "wine", and "pass" appear here. It is no wonder that this poem has become the most touching farewell poem, not to mention the imagination of the expression "In yellow dust the sounds disappear" as follows:

In spring, second or third moon, oh,
Willows are green, and peaches red grow.
Carts and horses can't the song hear;
In yellow dust the sounds disappear.[45]

As for the preceding farewell poem, the travellers' emotions in the "inn", the "thriving" business, together with the ingenious ideas in the last two lines, are interwoven into a trifold singing of the Sunny Pass in the town of Weicheng. From then on, "Weicheng" is endowed with a distinctive poetic sense, as can be seen below:

A monk looks for a ferry to Mount Wu;
Wild geese fly into Weicheng in sunset.[46]

---

43 He Xun. "Farewell"; Wang Changling. "Farewell to Xin Jian at the Lotus Building"; Li Qi. "Farewell to Liu Yu"; Du Mu. "Tomb-Sweeping Day"; Wei Zhuang. "Taicheng".
44 Wang Wei. "Seeing off Yuan the Second to Anxi" (or "Song of Weicheng").
45 Xie Shang. "Song of the Main Roads".
46 Wei Zhuang. "In Qianyang County".

Language of the Tang poetry 85

In this way, poetry and life are repeatedly interwoven, enriching the vocabulary of poetry. With heroic faith in life and sensitivity to new things, poets in the Tang Dynasty absorb and create these words, thus making the language of poetry simpler and more profound. The peak of the Tang poetry comes into being quite creatively. There are neither allusions nor fancy phrases, neither imitation nor refinement. It seems that life itself is poetry. Of course, a fresh and rich vocabulary does not necessarily lead to good poems. There are also many bad poems in the Tang Dynasty. What determines a good poem is still its thoughts, feelings, and artistic achievement, the last of which is an intangible quality rather than a specific imitation. It is at the forefront in creativeness, not intended to be picked off the bookshelf. However, since language is the only medium of poetry, it directly affects the development level of the poetry circle, and the enrichment process of vocabulary belongs to the poeticisation of the language in the Tang poetry. The examples shown above are chosen randomly to describe the problems for convenience; thus, they might be biased as they are collected bit by bit from different resources.

This introduction just puts forward the above arguments on the achievements of the Tang poetry in terms of language for the reader's reference. Some of the opinions might be underdeveloped and need more research. As for today's poetry circle, what kind of poetic form, poetic language, and vocabulary will appear? Such questions could only be answered through our diligent writing practice. The past experience is at best for reference only, and the development of the national artistic form will never be repeated in history. New ways are waiting for people to explore, with the development of society, the development of life, and the development of language. New poetry has its own vast world. Let the traces of life, the broadcasting of radios, and all kinds of new things of our time pour into our hearts, and turn into poetic language, with images as its flying wings. One day, our poetry circle will be shining with more splendid colours unprecedented in any other times in history.

4 November 1963

Originally published in *Literary Criticism*, 1964 (1), entitled "On the Language of the Tang Poetry", with the author's own revision

6 Metrical patterns of the Tang poetry

The Tang Dynasty is the most prosperous period of classical Chinese poetry, of which the poetic forms based on ancient Chinese literary language—classical Chinese—developed to a very mature stage. In this period, the "age of five- and seven-character", the main genres are five-character ancient poems, seven-character ancient poems, five-character regulated poems, seven-character regulated poems, five-character quatrains, and seven-character quatrains. The four-character form of ancient times only occasionally appeared in *yuefu* ballads, which are basically five- or seven-character in the Tang Dynasty, and the four-character form is just a kind of leftover. For example, an ancient *yuefu* ballad "Dredging Alone" originally has four-character lines:

独漉独漉，水深泥浊；泥浊尚可，水深杀我。[dúlù dúlù, shuǐshēn nízhuó; nízhuó shàngkě, shuǐshēn shāwǒ.] (Trampling the mud alone, / In deep, muddy water. / Muddy water is fine; / Deep water kills me.)

However, in Li Bai's "Dredging Alone", they become five-character lines:

独漉水中泥，水浊不见月；不见月尚可，水深行人没！[dúlù shuǐzhōngní, shuǐzhuó bújiànyuè; bújiànyuè shàngkě, shuǐshēn xíngrénmò.] (I trample the mud alone. / Deep water shows no moon. / No moon is not bad; / The deep water kills passersby!)

Nevertheless, there are also four-character lines in the same poem:

罗帷舒卷，似有人开；明月直入，无心可猜。[luówéi shūjuǎn, sìyǒu rénkāi; míngyuè zhírù, wúxīn kěcāi.] (The curtain's rolled up, / Opened by any one? / The bright moonlight shines / On my pure heart.)

These are also Li Bai's famous lines. It can be seen that excellent works in the Tang Dynasty can be written in the four-character form; however, this is an exception, and a poem totally of four-character lines seldom appeared. The form of *Chuci* after four-character poetry also occasionally appeared in

Metrical patterns of the Tang poetry 87

the Tang Dynasty. For example, the form in "Nine Songs" is used in many famous poems such as Wang Wei's "Song of the Goddess Temple at the Fish Mountain", "Song of Ascending a Tower", and "Looking at the Zhongnan Mountains: A Song for the Imperial Secretary Xu", the last of which, a short poem, is quoted here:

晚下兮紫微，怅尘事兮多违；驻马兮双树，望青山兮不归。[wǎnxià xī zǐwēi, chàng chénshì xī duōwéi; zhùmǎ xī shuāngshù, wàng qīngshān xī búguī.] (Staying late is the North Star, / Feeling sad for things against us. / I stop my horse at two trees. / Looking at the green mountains, I won't return.)

Through these lines, it seems that the form of *Chuci* with the use of "兮" functioning as a pause and musical note suddenly becomes active again. In fact, these are only occasional exceptions. We know these exceptional phenomena, and we know better that the reason why the five- and seven-character forms become the main forms of the Tang poetry with overwhelming excellence is not because of the prohibition of other forms, but the result of the free competition of different forms. Poets generally choose the five- or seven-character forms, and creatively enrich them, which is natural in the development of poetry.

In the Tang Dynasty, the five- or seven-character forms appear in ancient poems, quatrains, and regulated poems (usually of eight lines). In addition, there is an underdeveloped five-character long regulated form, commonly known as *pailü*, which is actually a remnant of the Qi and Liang poetry. Parallelism emphasised in the Qi and Liang Dynasties, a poem is often formed with parallel couplets every two lines, while the last two lines can be excepted. This form evolves into a long regulated form in the Tang Dynasty, while the difference is that in the Qi and Liang Dynasties the law of level and oblique tones is not fully grasped, so it is not very strict in this aspect. However, we all know that the Tang poetry only critically inherited the poems since the Qi and Liang Dynasties because they required more natural and vigorous content and forms than those of the Qi and Liang Dynasties. Therefore, the relatively weak long regulated form, which totally originated from the Qi and Liang Dynasties, was undeveloped in the Tang Dynasty except in examination poetry or ordered poetry. In other words, it almost did not produce any excellent works.

The main achievements of the Tang poetry are ancient poems, quatrains, and regulated poems. First, regulated poetry, relatively complex in form, can be divided into five-character and seven-character regulated poems. A regulated verse consists of eight lines of five or seven characters in strict rhythm from beginning to end. Because the rhythm of every line in classical poetry is very obvious, it is unnecessary to write in separate lines. In fact, a complete poetic line usually forms a sentence. The eight lines in a poem can be divided into two parts. The middle four parallel lines must have antithesis while the four lines at the beginning and the end need not necessarily have

88   *Metrical patterns of the Tang poetry*

antithesis, even though they may form natural antithesis. Du Fu's "Missing Li Bai in Spring" notes:

> Li Bai's poems are invincible,
> Unconstrained and extraordinary,
> As fresh as Minister Yu Xin,
> As rare as Councillor Bao Zhao.
> In the Wei North, the spring trees stand;
> At the River East, the late clouds fly.
> When together can we drink a cup
> And enjoy a discussion with you?

Here, if we read the four lines at the beginning and the end together, we have "Li Bai's poems are invincible, / Unconstrained and extraordinary. / When together can we drink a cup / And enjoy a discussion with you?" Often the four lines form the poem's distinct theme, and the four lines forming two couplets in the middle enrich it; the former seems to be the backbone, while the latter are muscles or branches. Therefore, famous lines on scenery usually appear here in regulated poems. The reason why this kind of regulated poems is better than long regulated poems is that too many couplets exist in long regulated poems, which often produce too many muscles or branches. However, in regulated poems, their distribution is appropriate.

The last two lines, whether in regulated poems or long regulated poems, are generally not antithetical, because antithetical couplets are not suitable for strong concluding remarks. However, there are also occasional exceptions, such as Du Fu's "On the Army's Recapturing of Henan and Hebei":

> North of Ji reseized, I was at Sword Gate.
> When I heard it first, my tears stained my clothes.
> O, my wife and children had no sorrow;
> I rolled up the classics in a wild state.
> In broad days we drink hard and loudly sing.
> We'll return to our native land in spring.
> From Gorge Ba to Gorge Wu, our boat will go
> Through Xiangyang to Luoyang with no stop.

This is what Du Fu wrote in Zizhou, Sichuan, where he heard the news of the war being pacified and decided to return to Luoyang. The "Sword Gate", or the Jianmen Pass, refers to the Sichuan region. "North of Ji reseized, I was at Sword Gate. / When I heard it first, my tears stained my clothes" shows his tears of joy. "O, my wife and children had no sorrow; / I rolled up the classics in a wild state" shows his rapture after he composed himself. This is the first spring of the Guangde period (763–764) with peaceful atmosphere and great spring scenery, so that "In broad days we drink hard and loudly sing. / We'll return to our native land in spring". How to return to the native land? The poet is eager to make a plan for his journey, that is, "From Gorge

Metrical patterns of the Tang poetry 89

Ba to Gorge Wu, our boat will go / Through Xiangyang to Luoyang with no stop". Actually, the last two lines form a couplet, which generally cannot be at the end of a poem, but Du Fu made a wonderful and powerful ending in this poem through this special "complementary couplet", which is extraordinary and admirable in regulated poems.

However, it is not necessarily a regulated poem that only conforms to the law of antithesis. For example, another poem "Admiring Mount Tai" by Du Fu states:

> How about Mount Tai called Daizong?
> Qi and Lu mounts' green is endless.
> Nature makes them magic and fair,
> The South and North at dusk and dawn.
> In my breast, cloud layers rise up.
> I break my eyes to see birds back.
> Let's climb to the top of Mount Tai,
> And see how small the mounts will be!

Here the middle four lines are couplets, but the poem is a five-character ancient poem rather than a five-character regulated poem because there is another law of level and oblique tones in a regulated poem, which is not observed in the eight poetic lines. The law of level and oblique began to be deliberated also in the Qi and Liang Dynasties. At that time, it was called "four tones and eight diseases". That is, eight commandments were stipulated mainly through four tones. The central requirement of these eight commandments was to avoid monotonous repetition. By the Tang Dynasty, it was summed up as a law of level and oblique. If we obey this law, we will feel that the tones are more harmonic and smooth, and the sounds formed by a regular arrangement of level and oblique tones are like a calm wave, undulating harmoniously. Level tones include the equivalent of the first and second tones we speak of today, such as "欺[qī] (cheating)" and "旗[qí] (flag)". Oblique tones include the equivalent of the third and fourth tones we speak of today, as well as the shorter incoming tones in the ancient sounds, such as "起[qǐ] (up)", "器[qì] (utensil)", and "漆[qī] (lacquer)". Words of level tones are higher in pitch and can be lengthened, so they are relatively bright and clear; words of oblique tones are lower in pitch, and its pronunciation cannot be lengthened, thus relatively reluctant and low-pitched. That is the reason why regulated poems usually rhyme in level tones. The following four kinds of regulated poems can be formed by alternatively arranging the level (L) and oblique (O) tones:

five-character poem	seven-character poem
OOLLO	OOLLOOL
LLOOL	LLOOLLO
OLLOO	OLLOOLL
LOOLL	LOOLLOO

90　*Metrical patterns of the Tang poetry*

However, in order to be less rigid in use, these standard lines have a flexible rule, which is "being flexible at the first, third, and fifth words, while being rigid at the second, fourth and sixth words". That is to say, the second, fourth, and sixth words of a poetic line must abide by the standard law, while the first, third, and fifth words may as well be used flexibly. Naturally, a simpler law comes into being, merging the four kinds into two kinds. If we use the symbol Ⴆ to represent the flexible words, then the two patterns are:

five-character poem	seven-character poem
ႶOႦLႦ	ႶOႦLႦOႦ
ႦLႦOႦ	ႦLႦOႦLႦ

Of course, the last word of a rhymed line generally has a level tone as said before, so the last word of an unrhymed line naturally has an oblique tone. This simplified law can show more clearly the basic law that a level tone and an oblique tone should take turns in appearance. These second, fourth, and sixth words seem to be a few points fixed on something with a few pins, and the rest are not far away even though there might be differences. Of course, it is still not serious if there happens to be a little bit of discord on the second, fourth, or sixth words in writing a poem, but that is only an exception.

As for the relationship of level and oblique tones between lines, the law is that every two lines are regarded as a couplet. If the second, fourth, and sixth words in the first line are OLO, then those of the second line are LOL. The phonetic antithesis of level and oblique tones is also combined with the antithesis of the word meaning; the antithesis convention of meaning is "space" vs. "space" (for example, heaven vs. earth, far vs. near), "time" vs. "time", "plant" vs. "plant" (flowers vs. grass), and "animal" vs. "animal" (birds vs. fish), which are in fact a kind of comparison of similar things, while level and oblique tones are mainly contrasts. In other words, with the opposing tones of different nature, the similar repetition is adjusted, not falling into monotony. As for the relationship between each adjacent couplet, the second, fourth, and sixth words of adjacent lines (for example, the second and third lines) are exactly the same in tones, which causes the repetition of tones of the same nature. Because the third line is quite different from the second line in meaning, they need to have a closer relationship in level and oblique tones. Therefore, if it does not meet this requirement of similarity, it is called "loss of bond".

The antithesis in meaning and the regularity in level and oblique tones are the general characteristics of regulated poetry. However, Cui Hao's "Yellow Crane Tower" is an exception:

The immortal has flown away on the yellow crane,
Leaving here an empty Yellow Crane Tower to date.
The yellow crane has gone and never comes again.
For a thousand years, only the white clouds await.

Metrical patterns of the Tang poetry   91

Trees at the Hanyang town stand by the shining shore;
The Parrot sandbar has grass in the lush, green state.
After sunset, where can I find my home of yore?
The misty Yangtze River brings me longing great.

Without a strict metre in Chinese, it is still a masterpiece of seven-character regulated poetry. According to legend, the great poet Li Bai once climbed the Yellow Crane Tower. Viewing the beautiful scenery in front of him, he was enthusiastic with poetry writing. However, when he looked up, he saw Cui Hao's inscribed poem. Anyway, he could not think of a better poem. Finally, he had to write two lines about it: "The scene is remarkable but indescribable, / Because Cui Hao's poem is inscribed on top". It can be seen that even the best regulated poem is not necessarily the most strict with tones, parallelism, and antithesis.

The Tang poetry is best represented in the High Tang, when it reached the peak. However, the main achievement of the High Tang poetry is not in regulated poetry. As said before, the four lines at the beginning and end generally describe the theme more directly, while the middle four lines develop it and make it more vivid. That's a good idea, of course. However, if every poem were written like this, it would inevitably be rigid, so that ideas would develop in fixed steps and easily become stereotyped. For example, the eight lines of a regulated poem were once divided into four steps: opening, developing, changing, and concluding. The first and second lines are "opening", the third and fourth are "developing", the fifth and sixth are "changing", and the seventh and eighth are "concluding", so that every two lines follow a fixed pace in development, which is unavoidably stringent. Therefore, the achievements of the Tang poetry are more in quatrains and ancient poems.

First, a quatrain is a four-line folk song popular in the Northern and Southern Dynasties. Quatrains are often sung in the Tang Dynasty, as in the story of "wall-drawing in an official residence", and the singing of Li Guinian at the banquet for the Royal Emissary to Jiangnan. The original Chinese quatrains generally follow the law of level and oblique tones, but not very strictly. For example, Wang Wei's "Seeing off Yuan the Second to Anxi" reads:

A morning rain has washed Weicheng so clean;
The inn looks thriving in fresh willows green.
My friend, raise a toast with wine! One more cup!
West of the Sunny Pass no friend cheers you up.

This poem, also known as the "Triple Singing of the Sunny Pass" or the "Song of Weicheng"), is the most famous farewell poem. Regarding the rule of level and oblique tones, the second line should be the same as the third. However, the opposite is true here. It was very casual in quatrains, but since the Tang Dynasty the law of level and oblique tones has been used to make

92 *Metrical patterns of the Tang poetry*

poetry more smooth. It is natural to make it read as pleasant as possible in the four short lines. As for antithesis, it is even more casual. Too many antithetical lines are inappropriate for quatrains that mainly emphasise natural utterances, such as Du Fu's "Four Quatrains" No. 3:

> Two yellow orioles are singing among green willows;
> A row of egrets is flying to the blue sky above.
> A window frames the west ridge snow of a thousand years.
> At gate moors a boat for Dongwu ten thousand *li* away.

Predecessors say that this is a "semi-regulated poem" rather than a quatrain. However, it has to be called a quatrain, though not a standard quatrain because it has too many antithetical lines. Like a folk song, a quatrain is usually short and lively with natural and enlightening thoughts; it seems to arouse infinite imagination through a little enlightenment. For example, Wang Changling's "Boudoir Complaint" introduces:

> A young wife in her boudoir knew no grief.
> In spring she's dressed to mount a tower green.
> Seeing willows by the roadside, she'd blame
> Herself for urging her husband for fame.

This poem, inspired by the willow colour in spring, arouses all the thoughts and feelings of recruited husbands and their wives missing them. Another example is "A Song of the Northwestern People", also called "A Song of Geshu":

> The northern seven stars are hanging high;
> A Geshu rides with a broadsword at night.
> The strong horses and herdsmen up to now
> Would never dare to invade Lintao.

Here, with the simple image of Geshu Han, the whole solemn and vast scene of the frontier is evoked in this poem, which is actually a folk song.

Therefore, a quatrain is like throwing a stone into the water, which creates not only a spray but also a series of ripples; it is also like a verdant peak thrusting into the sky, making us naturally think of the continuous mountains. A quatrain only has four lines. However, it seems not too short because it breaks through a little bit and develops in an all-round way; without this effect, a quatrain will lose its characteristics. A quatrain is such a natural and meaningful form of poetry. Alternatively, it is the simplest poetry; it allows neither too much processing nor storytelling. As if with a knack, the window of poetry is suddenly opened. This genre is especially developed in the Tang poetry, which is remarkably enlightening.

Metrical patterns of the Tang poetry 93

Generally speaking, ancient poems are not strict in tones and antithesis. However, five-character ancient poems are different from seven-character ones in that the latter have more consideration in the two aspects, which are natural, not the law. Ancient poems are generally long, while a few are short. For example, Wang Wei's "Farewell" has only six lines:

> I dismount for a drink of wine,
> "Hi, my friend, where are you going?"
> You say for the unpleasant life,
> You'll retire by the South Mountains.
> Take care! I will not ask again.
> The white clouds there are without end.

Li Bai's "Song of Resting Crows" also has only seven lines:

> When the crows rest on the Terrace Gushu,
> Fair Xishi gets drunk in the palace of Wu.
> Wu songs and Chu dances are on for fun;
> The gray mountain is hiding half a sun.
> How the silver arrow times gold clock water
> Till the autumn moon sinks into the river!
> The East grows bright; rapture returns never!

However, generally speaking, middle or long ancient poems are the majority.

With an early origin, five-character ancient poems have been predominant in the 200–300 years from the Jian'an era to the Qi and Liang Dynasties. Of course, the language may be more popular and more fluent in the Tang Dynasty. However, because of its earlier origin, it retained the primitive and plain style. Generally speaking, five-character ancient poetry is the most simple and straightforward genre in the Tang poetry. For example, Du Fu's famous lines in "The Song of Feelings on Leaving for Fengxian County from the Capital" are:

> In red doors wine and meats are stale;
> On trails are frozen human bones.

The language is very simple and plain, with no antithesis. Moreover, the second line in the original Chinese has five words of the same oblique tone, which can only be in five-character ancient poems. Neither regulated poems nor quatrains can have such tones, nor can seven-character ancient poems. Moreover, this becomes a characteristic of five-character ancient poetry, which makes it more low-pitched. Thus, oblique tones are far more frequently used in five-character ancient poems than in any other genres. As said before, oblique tones are low-pitched while level tones are high-pitched; regulated poems usually rhyme with level tones, and seven-character

94 *Metrical patterns of the Tang poetry*

quatrains are the same, whereas many five-character quatrains rhyme with oblique tones. For example, Meng Haoran's "Spring Dawn" reads:

Spring sleep is woken at dawn hours
When birds are chirping there and here.
The night wind and rain in my ear,
Fallen are how many flowers?

Here we can see the difference between five-character and seven-character quatrains. The former developed earlier, while the latter developed 300–400 years later until the Sui and Tang Dynasties. Thus, five-character quatrains are more plain and antique than seven-character ones. Especially five-character ancient poems, which directly inherited the earlier tradition of ancient poetry, are plain and clear from tones to language expressions. The five-character ancient poetic form was used in most of Du Fu's bitter poems reflecting the suffering of the time, such as "Three Officers", "Three Separations", "Northern Expedition", and "The Song of Feelings on Leaving for Fengxian County".

As it was formed relatively earlier, five-character ancient poetry is relatively farther from the *yuefu* ballads in the Han and Wei Dynasties. Although it was originally developed from *yuefu* ballads, the more refined and rigorous development process actually made it distinct from it. The *yuefu* ballads in the Tang Dynasty appeared less in five-character ancient poetic form. For example, most of Li Bai's *yuefu* ballads are seven-character, while his ancient poems are five-character. This shows that five-character ancient poetic form is one of the most ancient poetic styles in the Tang poetry. It is a long-matured genre with five characters in each line from beginning till end, so it does not feature the miscellaneous-character form common in *yuefu* ballads. On the one hand, it is simple. On the other, it is relatively solemn, forming a low-pitched and rigorous style. These are the features of five-character ancient poetry.

Seven-character ancient poetry is much younger than five-character ancient poetry. It is not developed into a genuine form until the Sui and Tang Dynasties. Calling it ancient poetry is only to differentiate it from regulated poetry and quatrains. Moreover, it grew up under the influence of stressing the parallel beauty, rhyme, and rhythm in the Qi and Liang Dynasties, and appeared in the form of chanting poems in the Chen and Sui Dynasties. In the Early Tang, it was obviously influenced by the Qi and Liang styles. It was not until the High Tang that it completely got rid of that influence and became the most unconstrained genre. It was not until the Tang Dynasty that it became fully mature; thus, as in modern poetry, it naturally had the features of regular level and oblique tones and antithesis, which are considered a free use of the characteristic of poetic language rather than a metrical form.

Seven-character ancient poetry grew up from chanting poems, with a deep relationship with *yuefu* ballads. Therefore, miscellaneous-character

Metrical patterns of the Tang poetry 95

lines can be allowed. For example, five-, four-, and three-character lines, or even more changeable syntax might appear in the same poem. Li Bai's "Hard are the Trails of Shu" prominently shows this characteristic. Another example is Chen Zi'ang's "Song of Mounting the Youzhou Terrace":

> Before, no ancients were seen;
> After, no followers will be seen.
> How vast the sky and earth are;
> Alone, I feel sad and shed tears!

None of the lines is seven-character, but predecessors still classified the poem as a seven-character ancient poem, precisely because they have miscellaneous-character lines. However, such miscellaneous-character lines are not the majority. Even in *yuefu* ballads, they are also an absolute minority. What is more common is the addition of five-character lines in seven-character ancient poems. For example, Cen Shen's "Mounting the Ancient Ye City" reads:

> I dismount my horse to ascend Yecheng,
> But what is seen in the empty city?
> The eastern wind is blowing the wild flame;
> The sun sets in the Flying Cloud temple.
> The south city corner faces the Hill-View hall;
> The Zhang River flowing east returns not at all.
> All people in Emperor Wu's palace have gone.
> For whom spring colours come every year on and on?

Many excellent poems are written in such a form of four five-character lines followed by four seven-character lines. Although the number of both five-character and seven-character lines is four, it is still called a seven-character ancient poem. Another example is Li Bai's "Yang Rebel":

> You're singing "Yang Rebel", and I
> Urge you to drink the New Home wine.
> What I care about most? The crow
> Of black birds in the white-door willows.
> The birds are lost in the flowers, so
> You get drunk and stay at my home.
> In the double-hill stove when incense woods are burnt,
> A couple of smokes soars to the purple sunset.

Here six lines are five-character, and only the last two lines are seven-character, but it's also called a seven-character ancient poem.

More achievements of seven-character ancient poems lie in the longer ones. The sweeping changes and coherent style make the seven-character ancient form the most personalised and liberating. Generally speaking, poets good at writing seven-character ancient poetry tend to be unconstrained in personality because it is especially suitable for poets to experiment and develop their vigorous imagination. That's why images in "The Yellow River falls from the Heaven" appear in a seven-character ancient poem. This is exactly its characteristic.

Either five-character or seven-character ancient poems are allowed to change rhymes because of their long length. Especially in the latter, the changes of rhyme are more common.

Generally speaking, regulated poems are complicated, quatrains ethereal, five-character ancient poems low-pitched, and seven-character ancient poems unconstrained.

Of course, what's stated above are only their general characteristics, which are subject to changes and development according to the poetic contents in the poet's hands.

Originally published in *Chinese Learning*, September 1957

7 Vitality and new prototypes of poetry

If we pay attention to the vicissitude of the poetry circle, we will definitely find that the prototypes of poetry often change accordingly. The eternal Nature, which we call the treasure house of art, is also constantly changing in the poet's pen. This leads to all the history of poetry.

In fact, any new trend of poetry often has a new form, which may not be necessary, but always seems better than nothing. It is the fairest example that the five-character form that prevailed in the Wei, Jin, and Six Dynasties had to give in to the seven-character form even though it was still alive in the Tang Dynasty. We want to be new, then everything will be new, and everything will naturally bring forth the new through the old; creation, the trend of an era, will affect every corner of the earth more or less, which naturally makes the content more important than the form.

The content of a poem is originally taken from the most sentimental things in life, and the reason why "spring flowers" and "autumn moon" appear quite often in poems is that they are most easily felt. However, over time these sentimental things become clichés or a kind of moan without illness. Then, new and sentimental things become necessities in life. Confucius says, "If one can make it new for one day, he should make it new every day until the end of days". The most direct creation of a new poetic style is to attach new feelings to new things. This is the constant pursuit of poetry.

Let us start with new things. Music is the best in inspiring emotions, and the music of China can be represented by the *qin* zither, a five- or seven-stringed plucked instrument. *Shijing* suggests, "What a gentle and beautiful girl! / Play the zither to befriend her". Confucius heard in Wucheng the sound of strings that were certainly plucked string instruments such as the *qin* or *se* zither (a 25- or 50-stringed plucked instrument); Sima Xiangru stirred up Wenjun's love with his heart expressed with the zither and made her run away for him at night, demonstrating the unimaginable effect of the *qin* zither.

However, the "*qin*" zither has not had a poetic flavour until late in the Jian'an era. Cao Pi's "Song of the Yan" states: "I plucked the *qin* zither strings and played a sad song, / But short singing or soft chanting cannot last long". This is the beginning of the *qin* zither with poetic feelings. Then,

98 *Vitality and new prototypes of poetry*

it really became a poetic longing in Zuo Si's "Inviting Recluses": "There are rock caves but no houses. / In the hill a *qin* zither is plucked". Tao Yuanming kept a zither without strings and sometimes caressed it to express poetic feelings without plucking it, which can be regarded as a fairy tale about the *qin* zither. Since then, the *qin* zither has become a sentimental thing in poetry, as in Yu Xin's lines: "The *qin* zither's sounds fill the room; / Rolls of books pile up the bedhead". Moreover, Lu Zhaolin's poem personifies: "Mounts and rivers play the zither; / Breeze and flowers often make toasts". The zither in the poems has profound meanings. However, another new instrument, the Qiang flute of the Hu tribes, replaced it and became prominent. With far greater magic than that of the *qin* zither in poetry, the "flute" aroused people's love from "Plucking Willows" in the Northern Dynasties:

> You mount the steed, not for the whip,
> But for plucking willow branches.
> You dismount to play the Qiang flute;
> The sadness softly kills passers.

Since then, the sound of flute always seems to invite excellent poetic lines, as in Wang Changling's "On a hundred-foot tower west of the beacon, / I sit alone at dusk, facing the autumn sea wind. / When the Qiang flute is playing the 'Guanshan Moon', I / Feel more the boudoir's sorrow ten thousand *li* away", Wang Zhihuan's "The Yellow River rises far above the white clouds. / A lonely city stands before ten thousand mountains. / Why should the Qiang flute complain of willows? / The spring breeze does not break through the Yumen Pass", and Wang Wei's "A teenager swordman from the capital Chang'an, / Mounted the guard tower to watch the Star of War. / The moon far from Lin'guan shines above Longtou, / On which a soldier is playing the flute at night". These are masterpieces of a generation. As for "Lower-Yangtze soldiers sometimes pass by Yangzhou, / And play the flute before the ancient Lanling town. / Going back by night fires to the out-town Fuchun, / They hear storks cry in the Stone City in autumn wind", the sound of flute runs through in evoking readers' feelings. Moreover, how heart-stirring is Li Yi's "Hearing the Flute when Climbing the Surrendered City at Night" in stating that "The sand before the Huile Mounts is like snow; / Out of the City, the moon is frost-like. / No one knows where the reed pipe is playing, / But soldiers are missing their homes all night". The word "flute" worthy of a thousand gold coins thus becomes the pride of the poetry circle. If we say that the "*qin*" zither accompanies five-character poems, then the "flute" is a bosom friend of seven-character poems. It is not only a new form or a new thing but a new feeling. It often appears simultaneously with the poetic sense. The flute seems different from poetry, but the two are sometimes integrated into one. Thus, it becomes a prototype of poetry.

As for the new feeling, "Minor Court Hymns" says: "Of yore I went away, / Willows would not say bye. / Missing, I'm here today; / Both rain

Vitality and new prototypes of poetry   99

and snow come by". However, this seems to be only a temporary encounter with willows. Later, Han people pluck willows to bid farewell, as the *Yellow Map of Three Districts* states: "The Baqiao Bridge was built over water to the east of Chang'an City. Han people often see off their friends here and pluck willows to bid farewell". However, good poems about "willows" did not appear yet. Since Jian'an, the trees being first sung are actually the "mulberry", "sophora", "pine", "cypress", "white poplar", and so on. "Verdant grass grows along the river banks; / Green willows in the garden are flourishing" in the "Nineteen Ancient Poems" did not arouse any common interest either. Later, Lu Ji's "Imitating Ancient Poems" includes: "Cool breeze winds around the curved house; / Cold cicadas sing in tall willows". Tao Yuanming's "Imitating Ancient Poems" says: "Lush orchids grow under the window; / Plenteous willows are before the hall". His *Biography of Mr Five Willows* seems to have affection towards "willows". However, the true understanding of "willows" begins from the Northerners' "Song of Plucking Willows":

> Along the Mengjin River afar,
> Willows are green and luxuriant.
> Born in a Hu family,
> I know not Han people's songs.

It is out of expectation that the gentle and graceful willows were first described in a tough northern song. Moreover, the lyrics of "Plucking Willows" soon became a new interest in the literary circle. King Jianwen and King Yuan of the Liang Dynasty and so on also imitated after "Plucking Willows". Later, Xue Daoheng's "Singing Songs Every Night" describes: "The weeping willows grow on golden banks. / The seedling leaves are plenteous again". "A Farewell Poem" by an anonymous poet asks:

> Green weeping willow twigs fall on the ground.
> Catkins of willows are flying in the sky.
> All willows twigs plucked, catkins are not found.
> Who can tell me when wanderers come back?

Ever since, the real sentiment of "willows" is known. In Liu Xiyi's "A beauty in the bridal chamber / Looked back at the weeping willows" and Song Zhiwen's "At dawn I left the willow and poplar wind by the bridge. / At dusk I lied by Yi's peaches and plums under the moon", the poetic sense of the new sentiment is distinct without need to say anything.

In fact, if we really want to explain the change of prototypes, then we would better look directly at natural phenomena because poets since Jian'an have been good at writing about the "wind". For example, in "Dry mulberries knew the spring wind", "A high terrace has more sad wind", "Hu horses stand in the north wind", "White poplars receive more sad wind",

100 *Vitality and new prototypes of poetry*

"Strong wind blows away the white sun", "The North wind is strong and grievous", and so on, excellent lines with the "wind" are at their fingertips. However, few excellent works are about the "rain". The rain appeared before the Sui and Tang Dynasties in such lines as "The night rain dripped on vacant steps. / The dawn darkened the light in the room", and "On the dark river, the rain will come. / The early wind turns the waves white". The "rain" did not officially have a status in poetry until Wang Changling's lines such as "When cold rain came to River Wu at night, / I bid farewell at Mount Chu alone at dawn. / If my friends in Luoyang ask about me: / A piece of ice heart is in a jade pot" and "A lone boat faces maple woods under a new moon; / The zither is played to comfort wanderers' hearts. / Mountain colours fading in millions of raindrops, / A string is broken, and he concludes with sad tears". People must have wondered whether it was always sunny before the Tang Dynasty! Though the poetic sense of the "wind" has not diminished, the new sentiment of the "rain" has become much stronger, as shown in: "Mountain fruits are falling down in the rain; / Grass insects are chirping under the lamp", "Trees of yellow leaves in the rain; / A white-haired man under the lamp", "Little clouds crossing the River of Stars, / The drizzle is falling on plane trees", and "Chimes of the Long Joy cease outside the flowers. / The rain greens the willows by the Dragon Pond". In Du Mu's "In the Tomb-Sweeping days, the drizzle falls endlessly, / All travellers on the road seem to have lost their souls", the sentiment and flavour of the "rain" are likely to penetrate everyone soul; in Li He's famous lines: "Young as these people are, it's near the dusk. / Peach blossoms are falling like the red rain", the "rain" becomes another prototype of poetry in a new way. We admit that the wind and the rain are two things. However, we may as well look at the vicissitudes of one prototype. Since the Wei and Jin Dynasties, the "sunset" has been called "the white sun" as in "The white sun runs towards the West", "The white sun falls into the West", "The white sun vanished in the West", "Farther away the chariot goes; / Darker the white sun slowly turns", and "The white sun gilds the soaring roofs; / Mansions in the city are seen". It was not until Wang Zhihuan's "The white sun hides behind high hills; / The Yellow River flows into the sea" that it came to the end of a period. Gradually the "sunset" was used in poems. For example, Wang Wei describes: "Pine and fir trees by the waterfall have raindrops / That turn to haze when the sun sets on the greenness". Meng Haoran depicts: "The sunset passing the West Mountains, / Groups of valleys turn dusky soon"; and Liu Changqing narrates: "Autumn geese fly ten thousand *li*; / Thousands of peaks share the sunset". Moreover, one of Wang Wei's famous quatrains describes:

> Grey is the temple in bamboos,
> The bell sound clear and deep at dusk.
> With a hat in the slanting sunset,
> He returns alone to green mounts.

Vitality and new prototypes of poetry 101

The poetic sense of the "sunset" completely changed when Li Shangyin sighs that "The sunset is gorgeous, / Only that it's near dusk". Since then, the "sunset" and the "slanting sunset" have become prototypes of poetry. In this way, we often produce new prototypes in what we have never noticed before. For example, the "pass" rarely appeared in poems before the Tang Dynasty. However, almost every poem related to the "pass" was excellent in the Tang Dynasty. Why wait until the Tang Dynasty to write such good lines as "In the passes of Han under the moon from Qin"? In addition, other lines such as "The spring breeze does not break through the Yumen Pass", "West of the Sunny Pass no friend cheers you up", "A harsh frost fell on the elm trees of the pass last night", and "The sun shines on the Tongguan Pass of four opened gates" also became masterpieces. On the contrary, our favourite things are not necessarily poetic. People in the Six Dynasties were fond of drinking, but almost no poetic "wine" was written in that period. Tao Yuanming is said to have the "wine" in each of his poems, and he should have written good poems on it. However, though his poems entitled "Drinking Wine" have good lines, they are not related to the "wine", as in "Chrysanthemum picked at the Eastern fence, / The southern mountain shows up, carefree". The wine is so familiar to people, but for a long time it is only taken as a topic, or appears as a good enjoyment of life, as in "Drinking spring wine with happy talks; / Picking fresh greens in my garden" and "New voices are heard in clear songs; / Green wine makes pretty faces smile". Although they are good lines, the wine is nothing more than itself. However, Wang Han toasts, "The grape wine glows in luminous jade cups. / Drink! But the *pipa* calls horseback lineups". Wang Wei urges, "My friend, raise a toast with wine! One more cup! / West of the Sunny Pass no friend cheers you up". Li Bai sighs, "Cut water with a sword, it faster flows. / Drink wine to ease sorrow, it deeper grows" and "The endless fine wine in Baling / Kills the Dongting autumn drunken". Du Fu describes, "For compiling, candles are burnt short. / Gazing at swords, we drink wine long". Then, the wine seems to be a poetic catalyst for the unsaid rapport. Even "Bringing in the Wine" thus became a well-known *yuefu* ballad. Since then, with Du Mu's "When I asked a cowboy where to find a wine house, / He fingered at the Apricot Bloom village far" and Wei Zhuang's "Cherish the host's kind heart because / More wine shows deeper affections", it is not open to question whether the "wine" has become a new prototype of poetry or not.

In the Tang Dynasty, not everyone is a genius, but poets appear one after another, precisely because at that time new poetic prototypes are found the most. Regarding the aforementioned prototypes, Wang Wei's "Song of Weicheng" has to be an excellent poem, because each line has one of the new prototypes concerning the "rain", "willow", "wine", and "pass". Moreover, the new prototypes were never confined to these few because they were common in life at that time. If we were born in the Tang Dynasty, and if we were to discover new prototypes at that time, then would we have not created a

102   *Vitality and new prototypes of poetry*

good line or two at our fingertips? However, such a high time of poetry writing did not come by itself. If no one had discovered these new prototypes, they would have never been found. The Tang people did take advantage of it because people in the Six Dynasties were constantly discovering, and the peak of discovery was reached just in the Tang Dynasty. But, who would first discover them while we are waiting? Today, as we are not able to take advantage of the predecessors, we would better generously leave a little legacy for future generations. What's more, it is no good to take too much advantage. When the Song people inherited from the Tang people, prototypes such as the wine, rain, willow, flute, mountain, water, slanting sunset, and verdant grass were too messed up to do anything. That is why *ci* poetry (also lyrics) is only a poetic remnant, even though it has several treasured prototypes such as the "mansion" in "The twilight shines in tall mansions", the "bridge" in "Riding a horse on a slant bridge", the "catkin" in "Weeping willows and falling catkins filled the eyes", the "swing", and the "railing". They support a period of life for *ci* poetry; however, having too many ready-made prototypes limited its development. Li E of the Sui Dynasty reports, "A long list of writings was all about the moon and dewdrops. Many cases of books were only concerned with the wind and cloud". However, the Tang people were not limited to such prototypes as the "wind and cloud" and the "moon and dewdrops". Thus, they were perfect in accomplishing what had been expected in the Six Dynasties. Today, we are not able to take advantage of the Six Dynasties like the Tang people, nor should we be like the Song people fed up with the Tang people. Besides, we are in a changing era in which everything keeps changing. For example, the "wine" that people used to drink has become the "smoke" now. The "horse" that people used to ride has become the "bicycle". These changes are the best place to discover new prototypes of poetry. For example, the house where I live now had a very quiet environment, but it is too close to the airport. From morning till night, the roar of planes' engines outside the window always made me really frustrated. I was disturbed very much at first and even hated this material civilisation. However, I soon found that I was doing wrong because if I considered the noise irreconcilable and continued to hate it, there would be only two results: either I finally destroy the plane, or the plane finally destroys me. I thought I was probably not able to destroy the plane, which was undoubtedly a tragic thing. However, a poet says:

I hear the factory sirens calling the workers.

What a joyful sound it is! Since then, I learned a lot about emotional stubbornness. We have deep prejudices about old emotions and cannot discover new ones. The so-called beauty of quietness and seclusion is just the feeling we inherited from our predecessors, and it should not become a habit in our lives. For example, all kinds of wires of the streetcars, lamps, and telephones

Vitality and new prototypes of poetry   103

in the city are crisscrossed, which is a kind of trouble from the old emotional point of view; however, a poet says:

The floating wires are like a musical score.

How gratifying this feeling is! We must let all things in the world have the breath of life together so that we do not fall into mechanical boredom because of material civilisation. It is precisely because of the rapid progress of science that literature and art seem to be caught off guard and lose the joy and reasons of life. We almost blindly go along with material conditions. The theme of all things today is how we can always have new emotions in our lives, and always be affected by the tide of emotions. Our feelings towards new prototypes of poetry have a long history and will take us a long way. Today we should be the pathfinders because we seem to have no ready path to follow. However, we are walking into a new era in which many things are not what they used to be, just as the "paths" that used to be regarded as a symbol of sorrowful parting in poetry has become the "paths" of union and joy because of developed transportation. These are all new developments. Now let me introduce another poetic stanza:

The hoes in spring are the sound of the earth.
The footsteps of spring are the sound of roads.
Will you write to the road builders?
For the first time, spring is in your letter.

We write poetry to extend the history of poetry because each time we discover a new prototype, we write a new poetic line for the history of poetry. A radioactive prototype certainly cannot create an atomic age, but the atomic age is being created by the continuous discovery of new prototypes. They seem to be separated from each other, but become a power when integrated together. This is a historical force that illustrates the essence of poetry.

If we think the universe has a long history, then, of course, the history of human beings is very short by comparison. However short it is, the history of human creation is not different from that of universe creation. Both of them need power, which has been decided since the beginning. Just as a seed sprouts and grows, changing in different environments, the power behind it remains unchanged. I am earnest to emphasise that this power is the vitality of poetry.

If we compare any history with a play or a novel, the latter is, of course, much tinier. They are all stories with a beginning and an end, but the former is still developing whereas the latter is complete. Any history is a part of the whole history, but a great story is complete. Rather, it is not only complete but independent. If a poem is the shortest story, then we might as well say that a poem is the most complete history.

104 *Vitality and new prototypes of poetry*

It takes quite a long time for primitive men to advance to civilised ones. Nevertheless, in their minds, there must have been a force of attraction, just like the force tempting moths to fly to a flame. The power of light guided the barbarians into civilisation. Bare-handed, they walked into the civilised world. How strong this force was! They revealed the prelude to civilisation only with their naturally endowed bright eyes, intelligent ears, and flexible perceptions. This vivid development teaches the highest of all arts and tells the reason why all complex arts with trivial details are finally lacking in achievement. For the countries of ancient cultures in history, their tragic fate of decline is often unavoidable. Thus, this is the high time we seek creativity, in which we find the essence of poetry. That is why new prototypes of poetry keep emerging.

In the long line of historical development, its power initially lies at only a point. The longer the line is pulled, the weaker its creativity is. The shorter the line becomes, the stronger its creativity is. If the line is as short as a point, it becomes the creativity itself. As light can be focused at a point, the artist makes history a focal point. In this way, a play or a novel shortens the whole history to a story. Poetry is the highest of all arts because it is the true embodiment of that point.

However, a point always develops into a line. The value of art is to remedy natural shortcomings; it is thus interpreted as a craft. When history has developed into a line, art can convert it into a point, which was originally focused in the primitive time, and is now focused in any time. Poetry is an endless language because its background is the endless history.

If we did not have primitive interests, we would not have had the most progressive culture because they need the same historical starting point; literature and art, therefore, do not await but create the time. Thus, poetry is a lofty feeling of the time. Seven years ago, I passed by a town called Hetian, where all the hills were bare without trees, and the soil on the hills was gradually deserted because there were no trees to protect it, so they looked like bald heads from a distance. As I passed by the hills, I was greatly impressed by the sight of a few small pine trees. They were probably specially planted by the agricultural and forestry operations, but looked like a group of poor underdeveloped children. It was simply a struggle. If the small pine trees could not save the barren hill, they would die. It resembles the phenomenon in our culture today.

I do not want to brag about our civilisation lasting for more than 5,000 years. In fact, our ancient civilisation is facing a difficult problem today. On the one hand, ancient civilisations indisputably have a glorious history; on the other, they are inevitably prone to ageing. How many of the earliest ancient civilisations in the world can still remain strong among the world's advanced ranks? We are at the renewal stage of our ancient history; thus, poetry has to strive with all its might in this age, just like the little pine trees planted on the deserted hills. "In the vast desert a lone smoke rises up; / In the long river the setting sun is full". Poetry is, therefore, a call to life, enlivening all the lifeless with the source of life, and awakening the feelings of life in all the most uninteresting places. The vitality of poetry, a creation of the whole history, must be achieved from the lowest to the loftiest; poetry is therefore the voice of the universe, and this is the high time that new prototypes emerge continuously. How will we sustain the vitality of poetry, and how will we develop new prototypes? The answers to the two questions will contribute to another era of poetry.

Originally published in *Literature Journal*, February 1948, 2(9)

Postscript to the Chinese edition

The Tang poetry is a glorious milestone in the history of ancient Chinese poetry. Its fresh artistic feeling, simple but profound language, vigorous atmosphere, and liberating sentiment all leave an unforgettable impression on people. It's impossible to inquire about the nature of this peak and to explore its mystery in a few words. Therefore, I tried to achieve some general understanding of the poetry in the High Tang from different perspectives. In this way, I wrote articles whenever I had ideas, some of which are relatively direct while others are relatively indirect. The first part is called "The Peak of the Tang Poetry" and the second part "Far Notes of the Tang Poetry", which are combined into the book *A Comprehensive Study of the Tang Poetry*. It includes "The Poet Li Bai" published as a book earlier. "Essays on Poems" at the book's end consists of 19 short essays, most of which were written in the early years on poems from the beginning of classical Chinese poetry to the Tang and Song Dynasties. Most of the essays are my understanding of a few poetic lines not worth serious discussion, which are included as the residual sound of the book.

The compiling of this book cost a long time in finding and reproducing the publications in newspapers and journals because nine out of ten of my manuscripts were lost in the Cultural Revolution (1966–1976). Zhong Yuankai and Shang Wei, postgraduate students at Peking University, have successively helped to complete this work. When the manuscript is published, I would like to express my deep gratitude to them. Hereby I conclude the postscript.

In Yannan Garden on 10 December 1985

Appendix
Mr Lin Geng's academic chronology[1]

Lin Geng, alias Jingxi, was born in Beijing on 22 February 1910 (the 13th day of the first lunar month) to a family from Minhou County (now in Fuzhou City), Fujian Province. His father is Lin Zhijun (1879–1960), alias Zaiping, a famous scholar and calligrapher who studied in Japan in his early years.

1928

Graduated from the High School Affiliated to Beijing Normal University; enrolled in the Department of Physics, Tsinghua University.

1930

Transferred to the Department of Chinese Language and Literature, Tsinghua University. Joined the "Chinese Literature Society" under Zhu Ziqing's guidance and founded with his poet friends a student magazine, *Literature Monthly*, in the Department of Chinese Language and Literature, Tsinghua University.

1931

Published in *Literature Monthly* 16 *ci* poems such as "To the Tune: Exotic Dancers Called Buddhists". Began to write new poems in free verse after writing ancient poems; wrote a new poem "Prayer at Twilight", which was published later in *Youth Music* in 1942 (Volume 2, No. 4), and made into music by Zhang Dinghe.

1932

Wrote for himself: "A little spark can start a fire that burns the entire prairie / Too much ash is useless / I will explore why a little spark burns a prairie / And trace the beginning of all beginnings", which became the motto of his constant exploration and transcendence in his studies and career.

---

1 This chronology is in reference to "The Annalistic Record of Lin Geng's Works" co-authored by Peng Qingsheng and Fang Ming.

108 *Mr Lin Geng's academic chronology*

1933

Graduated from the Department of Chinese Language and Literature, Tsinghua University; began working at Tsinghua as an assistant of Zhu Ziqing, and assessed students' homework in the course of Chinese for Wen Yiduo. At the invitation of Zheng Zhenduo, became an editor of the *Literary Quarterly*, responsible for soliciting contributions to the column on new poetry.

On 18 September, published his first new poetry collection *Night* at his own expense, for which Wen Yiduo designed the book cover, and Yu Pingbo wrote the foreword. This collection selected 43 new poems in free verse written from 1931 to 1933, including "Through the Mist" and "Night".

1934

At the beginning of the year, resigned from the teaching assistantship of Tsinghua University to prepare for professional writing. In spring, went to Shanghai, Nanjing, Suzhou, and so on, and became acquainted with writers such as Shi Zhecun and Mao Dun.

In summer, returned to Beijing; taught the History of Chinese Literature as a lecturer at the Peping Republic College.

In October, published his second poetry collection, *Spring Wilderness and Windows*, in the Peping Literature Review Press, for which his fiancée Ms Wang Xiqing painted the cover. This collection includes 57 new poems in free verse such as "Spring Wilderness", "Dawn", and "Nature".

Began to write new poems in metric rather than in free verse.

Set out to write *A History of Chinese Literature*.

1936

Continued to teach in the Peping Republic College, while teaching part-time at the Women's College of Arts and Sciences of Peping University, and Peping Normal University.

On 22 February, published *Peiping Love Songs*, his third collection of new poems in the Peiping Wind and Rain Poetry Society, including 58 new metrical poems such as "An Autumn Day", "Dream Talks by the Stove", and "Ancient Feelings".

In November, published *Hibernation Melody and Others*, his fourth collection of new poems in the Peiping Wind and Rain Poetry Society, for which Qiming (Zhou Zuoren) wrote the book title and Feiming wrote the foreword. This collection contains 32 new metrical poems such as "Hibernation Melody", "The First Lunar Month", and "Fine Drizzle", followed by the "Postscript" written on 1 November.

Had 19 new poems translated into English and collected in *Modern Chinese Poetry* (London, 1936), edited by British Professor Harold Acton.

1937

The Lugou Bridge (also the Marco Polo Bridge) Incident broke out, and the War of Resistance against Japan began. At the beginning of September, invited by Zhu Ziqing on behalf of Sa Bendong (also Adam Pen Tung Sah), President of Xiamen University, to teach as a lecturer. Went to Xiamen from Tianjin via Hong Kong on a British ship of the Swire Pacific.

1938–1940

In the summer of 1938, promoted to the associate professorship. Published articles "On the Xiang Legends" and "On the Forms of New Poetry".

1941

Promoted to the professorship.

Published in Xiamen University Press the first three mimeographed editions of *A History of Chinese Literature*: *The Age of Enlightenment*, *The Golden Age*, and *The Silver Age*. First proposed "the Youth Spirit in the Tang poetry" in "The Peak of the Poetic State", the 14th chapter of *The Golden Age*.

1942–1946

Published two new poems "Autumn Colours", and "A Dialogue at Dawn", as well as an article "A Random Talk on Teaching Selected Poems".

1947

Published *A History of Chinese Literature* in Xiamen University Press, for which Mr Zhu Ziqing wrote the foreword.

In summer, resigned from Xiamen University.

In autumn, returned to Peping and served as a professor at Yenching University.

1948

Wrote more than ten poems and articles. Put forward in "The Forms of New Poetry Revisited" for the first time the "half-pause law", insisting that a slight pause in a five-character or seven-character poem always divides the characters into either two-three, or four-three in terms of Chinese characters.

1949

From 2 to 29 July, participated in the First National Congress of Literary and Art Workers in China. Was a representative of each following congress.

110   *Mr Lin Geng's academic chronology*

In September, completed a long poem "People's Days", which was published in *Popular Poetry* in 1950 (Volume 1, No. 2).

1950

In May, participated in the First Congress of Literary and Art Workers in Beijing. On 31 May, made a speech at the closing ceremony, and was elected as a council member of the Beijing Literature and Art Federation.

1951

Published in *Guangming Daily* (also *Enlightenment Daily*) "Re-discussing Nine-Character Poems", "On the Idea that Content Determines Form—Answering Mr Pu Yang", and an article about Qu Yuan.

1952

Became a professor in the Department of Chinese Language and Literature of Peking University when Yenching University merged into Peking University in the national adjustment of institutions.

In August, published *A Study of Poet Qu Yuan and His Works* in the Bush Cherry (also Tangdi) Press.

1953

In June, attended on behalf of China the 2230th anniversary of the death of Qu Yuan, one of the Four Famous Men of World Culture, and gave a lecture "The Emergence of the Poet Qu Yuan", which was published in *Ta Kung Pao* on 13 June.

1954–1955

From 1 March on, served as an editor of the newly founded *Literary Heritage*, a supplement of *Guangming Daily* until June 1963 when it ceased publication.

In June, finished writing *The Poet Li Bai*, and made an academic report in the Department of Chinese Language and Literature of Peking University.

In September, published *A Brief History of Chinese Literature* (Upper Volume) in Shanghai Literature and Art United Publishing House. By November, it was reprinted three times totalling 10,000 copies.

In November, published in Shanghai Literature and Art United Publishing House *The Poet Li Bai*, which consists of 12 sections in five chapters and an appendix of 96 poems by Li Bai. In 1955, supplemented and revised the fourth section, and wrote a postscript for the third edition. From November

Mr Lin Geng's academic chronology 111

1954 to February 1958, it was printed seven times for circulation totalling 61,000 copies, which is rare in the research history of the Tang poetry. However, due to the overflow of "ultra-leftist ideological trend", his views have been constantly challenged and criticised.

1956–1957

In 1956, became the Director of the Teaching and Research Office of ancient literature in the Department of Chinese Language and Literature, Peking University. Served as the Director until retirement.

Peking University began to enrol doctorate students for Associate Doctorate Degrees, and Liu Xuekai became his first doctorate student for an Associate Doctorate Degree. In April 1957, gave the Advanced Party School Journalism Class an academic report entitled "A Bird's Eye View of Classical Chinese Literature", which was published in *Journalism and Publication*. In May, gave another academic report entitled "Four Greatest Tang Poets" in Qingdao. In the two years, published more than ten poems and articles.

1958

In summer, specially investigated and underwent "key criticism" when the nationwide "Educational Revolution" focused on criticising "Capitalist academic authorities" and "pulling out Capitalist white flags".

In winter, summoned for collaborative scientific research by the Central Government. Led with Mr You Guo'en some teachers in the Teaching and Research Office of ancient literature, Department of Chinese Language and Literature and the students of Class 4, Grade 56 to conduct studies on Tao Yuanming. In August 1961 and January 1962 respectively, two books, *A Collection of Research Materials on Tao Yuanming* and *Collected Reviews of Tao Yuanming's Poems and Essays*, were compiled and published by Zhonghua Book Company.

1959–1961

Published scores of poems and articles such as "Song in Early Autumn". Among them, "Yanshan and Heishan in the 'Song of Mulan'" published in *Wen Wei Po* on 1 April 1961 made a breakthrough in an unsolved problem.

1962

In January, published *A Collection of Research Materials on Tao Yuanming* in Zhonghua Book Company.

In March, co-edited with Chen Yixin and Yuan Xingpei and published in Zhonghua Book Company the upper and lower volumes of *Literature*

112   *Mr Lin Geng's academic chronology*

References of the Wei, Jin, Southern and Northern Dynasties, which were "selected and noted by the Teaching and Research Office of Chinese Literary History of Peking University".

1963–1965

Published five poems and articles, and edited the first and second books of the upper volume of *Selected Poems of all Dynasties in China*, which were published by the People's Literature Publishing House in January 1964.

1966–1972

Suffered in the "Cultural Revolution". Read *Journey to the West* at night.

1973

In April, published "An Analysis of the Battle of Red Cliff" in the *Journal of Peking University* (1973, No. 2). Later, it was included in *Talks on Journey to the West*.

1974–1982

Wrote nearly 20 poems and articles. In November 1979, co-edited and published the first and second books of the lower volume of *Selected Poems of all Dynasties in China* in the People's Literature Publishing House.

1983

In June, published in the People's Literature Publishing House *Commentaries and Notes on "Questions to Heaven"*, which consists of "Reading 'Questions to Heaven' Three Times" (preface), "Notes on 'Questions to Heaven'", "A Modern Language Version of 'Questions to Heaven'", and four articles related to the work.

Since this year, served as an editor of the *Encyclopaedia of China: Chinese Literature*, an honorary consultant of the *Chinese Education Dictionary*, and a consultant of the Chinese Society of Qu Yuan and the Association of Tang Literature of China.

1984

In June, published in Peking University Press *Asking for Directions*, which includes 109 new poems and 15 articles on new poems written from 1931 to 1981.

1985

In August, published in the People's Literature Publishing House *Lin Geng's Selected Poems*, which includes his 72 new poems from 1931 to 1981.

1986

Retired this year, but was still a doctoral supervisor in the Department of Chinese Language and Literature of Peking University.

1987

In April, published in the People's Literature Publishing House *A Comprehensive Study of Tang Poetry*. Prefaced with "Why Do I Particularly Love the Tang Poetry", it includes 21 articles such as "Chen Zi'ang and the Jian'an Spirit", "The High Tang Atmosphere", "Symbols at the Peak of the Tang Poetry", "Language of the Tang Poetry", "The Four Great Tang Poets", "The Poet Li Bai", "On the Artistic Reference of Classical Chinese Poetry" and "On 'Wooden leaves'"; and 19 articles on Tang poems such as "In the Wild There Died a Deer", "The Song of Yishui", "A Short Ballad", "In the Passes of Han under the Moon from Qin", and "On Meng Haoran's 'Passing by My Old Friend's Farmstead.'"

1988

In September, published a revised edition of *A Brief History of Chinese Literature* (Upper Volume) in Peking University Press.

1990

On 22 February, celebrated his 80th birthday. Wu Zuxiang wrote a scroll reading "Innocent as white snow, / As sunny spring as warm; / In sixty years, we know, / Your actions set the norm".

In August, published in the People's Literature Publishing House *Talks on Journey to the West*, which was noted by Shang Wei based on Lin Geng's oral instruction since 1987.

1991–1997

Published more than ten poems and articles. At the end of 1992, began to compile *A Brief History of Chinese Literature* (Lower Volume), which was published in Peking University Press in July 1995.

In August 1992, published *Tang Poems Recommended by Lin Geng* in Liaoning Children's Publishing House.

114 *Mr Lin Geng's academic chronology*

1998–1999

Published four articles, of which "From Free Verse to Nine-character Poetry" was published in *Literature, History and Philosophy* (1999, No. 3). It was later used as the preface of the book *Metrics of New Poems and the Poeticisation of Language*. This article reviewed the long history of new poetry creation over half a century from the 1930s to the 1990s, and summarised his creation practice and theoretical propositions on the forms of new poetry.

2000

In January, published the first edition of *The Poet Li Bai* in Shanghai Chinese Classics Publishing House.

In January, published in Peking University Press *Reverie in Space*, including 27 new poems unpublished before. Among them, 12 poems were interpreted with his proses.

In January, published in the Economic Daily Publishing House *Metrics of New Poems and the Poeticisation of Language*, which is one of the *Oriental Cultural Collections* edited by Ji Xianlin. This book includes the preface of *Asking for Directions* and 15 articles on poetry, three articles on new poems in *A Comprehensive Study of Tang Poetry*, "Nature of the Character '兮' in *Chuci*" in *A Study of Poet Qu Yuan and His Works*, and the articles on new poetry since 1995 including "Assumptions on New Poetry: Transplantation and Soil" and "From Free Verse to Nine-character Poetry" (preface), in addition to three interviews. They basically reflected Lin Geng's theoretical research on new poetry and his exploration of creating new poetry forms over the past 60 years.

In December, published "My Research on *Chuci*" in *Ways to Success in Chuci Studies: Reflections of International Chuci Experts* in Chongqing Publishing House. Based on the recordings and notes of Lin Geng's oral instruction, it was compiled by Dr Chang Sen from the Department of Chinese Language and Literature of Peking University, which was revised and finalised by Lin Geng.

2001

In October, published a seven-character regulated poem "On Li Bai" in *Knowledge of Literature and History*.

2002

On 4 April 2002, published a seven-character regulated poem "On Li Bai" in *People's Daily*.

In June, appointed as a consultant and the honorary president of the Chinese Society of Qu Yuan.

2003

Published an interview "The World is Searching for the Traces of Beauty" in *Literature and Art Research* (2003, No. 4).

2004

Appointed as the Director of the Poetry Centre of Peking University.

2005

In February, published nine volumes of *Lin Geng's Poetry and Articles* in Tsinghua University Press. Among them, Volume IX, *A Collection out of Collections* edited by Lin Geng himself, includes 90 individually published or unpublished poems, essays, articles, and interviews from 1931 to 2003. Lin Geng himself wrote the title of the book.

In November, published *A History of Chinese Literature* in Lujiang Publishing House.

2006

In September, invited by Peking University Press to publish *A Brief History of Chinese Literature* (with illustrations), which was finally published in August 2007.

On 4 October, bid farewell to life at the age of 97.

Index

An Shi Rebellion xiv, 3, 22–23, 51
Ancient Style 14, 18, 22–24, 36–37
art xi–xii, xiv, xvi, xviii, 1, 17, 36, 65,
   68–69, 71, 74, 77, 97, 103–104

Bai Juyi xxviii, 56
baihuashi 74
bamboo xx, 13, 30, 47, 62, 76
Bao Zhao 48, 64, 79–80, 88
Book of Songs see Shijing
border 18, 38, 51
bridge xiii, xx, xxii, 23, 71, 83, 99, 102

Cao Cao 2, 3, 6, 57, 65, 75, 79
Cao Pi xxiii, 48, 97
Cao Zhi 22, 31
Cen Shen 22, 95
characteristic i, xii, xx, 7–8, 18, 20, 33,
   37–38, 40–41, 47, 68–69, 73, 93–96
Chuci viii, x, xix, xx, xxviii, 37, 55, 57,
   67, 71–72, 79, 86–87, 114
ci poem xxii, xxvi, 107
ci poetry 102
classical Chinese poetry i, vi, ix, xvii, xix,
   xxi, xxii, xxv, xxvii, 2, 18, 20, 36, 38,
   41–42, 45–46, 67, 86, 106
commoner xiii
Confucius xix, 32–33, 43, 97
Cui Hao 25, 49, 90–91

Dongfang Qiu 10, 12
Du Fu xiii, xiv, xxiii, xxviii, 22, 38, 51, 56,
   61, 65, 67, 77, 83, 88–89, 92–94, 101
Du Mu 84, 100–101

Early Tang 3, 20–21, 25, 78, 94
exaggeration xv, 40, 67

Fan Li 58
five-character ancient poems xxv, 48, 86,
   93, 96

five-character quatrains 86, 94
flute xxii, 81, 98, 102
form iv, xiv, xvii, xviii, xix, xx, xxi, xxiii,
   xxv, 16, 39, 44, 46–47, 49, 55–57, 61,
   65, 69–73, 78–79, 82, 85–89, 92, 94,
   95–98
four-character xix, xx, xxv, 70–71, 79, 86
frontier fortress poetry xxiii, xxiv, xxviii,
   50–54, 80
fu xxvi, 7, 43–47, 67, 73, 79

Gao Shi 25, 37, 47, 53
Geshu Han 92
grass xxii, 12, 40, 45, 49, 56, 61, 63, 76,
   83–84, 90–91, 99, 102
gubaihua 69
Guo Pu 11
Gutishi 74–75

half-pause law xx, 109
Han and Wei Spirit 11, 24, 30
Han Yu 33
Hengjiang vi, vii, xv, 38, 65
hermit 57–59, 62
High Tang i, v, xii–xvii, xxiv, xxvii–viii,
   1, 2, 4, 16, 20–41, 48, 50, 52–53, 91,
   94, 106, 113
High Tang Atmosphere v, xii–xvii,
   xxvii–viii, 20, 23–29, 31–33, 36–37,
   39–41, 113
Huang Tingjian xxiii, 74–75
Huihong 74

image xv, xxii, xxiii, xxiv, 2, 12, 20, 25,
   27, 29, 36, 38–41, 65, 75–76, 83, 92

Jiang Kui xvi, 28
Jiangling 56, 58, 62
Jiangnan 4, 56–57, 63–64, 73, 81, 91
Jiangxia 50, 65
Jiaoran xvi

118 *Index*

Jinling 49
Jinshi 3, 43–44
Jintishi 74–75
Juren 6

Kaiyuan 3–6, 21–22, 25, 30, 50–51
Kongzi xix

landscape poetry v, xxiii, xxviii, 55–67, 75
language i, vi, ix–xi, xiii–xv, xvii–xxviii, 31, 33, 46–50, 54, 62, 66–69, 71, 73–75, 77–81, 84–86, 93–94, 104, 106
Laozi 58–59
Late Tang xiii, 1, 20, 30–31, 40
level x, xv–xvi, xxvi, 6, 39, 48–49, 65, 73–75, 78, 85, 87–91, 93–94
Li Bai vi, xiii, xv, xxviii, 8, 10, 14–15, 22–24, 26, 30, 36–39, 49, 51–52, 56, 65–67, 78, 86, 88, 91, 93–95, 101, 106, 110, 113–114
Li Guinian 52, 91
Li He 69, 100
Li Jinfa xxiv
Li Qi 5, 48, 84
Li Sao 12, 36
Li Shangyin 101
Liangzhou 61, 67, 80
Lin Geng i–v, viii–xxix, 19, 71, 107–115
Liu Changqing 100
Liu Fangping 40
Liu Yu 9, 63–64, 84
Liu Zhen 12–13, 26, 31
Longxi xiv
Lu Ji 45, 99
Lu Lun 40
Luoyang xv, 39, 47, 73, 88–89, 100

May Fourth New Culture Movement ix
Meng Haoran vi, xv, 30, 33, 66, 94, 100, 113
metrical pattern xxviii
Mi Yuanzhang 32
Mid-Tang xiii, xxvi, 20, 40
Minor Court Hymn xxii, 55, 83, 98
modern poetry xxi, 74, 94
moon xxii, 8, 16, 25–26, 34, 38, 40, 45, 51, 60–61, 65–66, 76, 80–84, 86, 93, 97–102

Nine Arguments xxiii
Nine Songs xx, xxii, xxiii, 36, 55, 63, 87
Nineteen Ancient Poems 61, 83, 99

oblique 48, 49, 87, 89–91, 93–94
Ode to the Orange xx, 12, 71

palace poetry 46, 56, 57, 61
Pan Xu 8
parallel prose xxvi, 46
pastoral poetry 60–61
patriotism 10
peak v, xii, xiii–xiv, xvii, xix–xxi, xxvi–vii, 1, 20, 22, 26, 34, 36, 39, 41–54, 69–73, 78–82, 85, 91–92, 102, 106
pipa 48, 101
poeticisation xviii, xix–xxviii, 69, 71–75, 78–79, 81, 83, 85
profundity xvi, xxiv–vi, 20, 28, 35, 37, 50, 68–69
prosification xviii
prototype 98, 100–101, 103

Qian Qi 43
Qiang flute 61, 98
qin zither 97–98
Qu Yuan viii, x, xxii–iii, 10, 12, 19, 36, 55, 71, 110, 112, 114
quatrain 31, 47, 52, 67, 91–92

rain vi, xv, xxii, 39, 47–48, 55, 57, 84, 91, 94, 98, 100–102
realism 1, 2, 14, 17, 19
regulated poem xxv, 44, 48–50, 86–89, 91, 93, 96, 114
River South *see* Jiangnan
romanticism xii, xvii, 1, 2, 7–10, 14, 16–19, 23, 36
Ruan Ji 11, 29–30

semi-regulated poem 92
seven-character ancient poems xxv–vi, 48–50, 53, 86, 93, 95–96
seven-character quatrains xxvi, 53, 86, 94
Shandong 4
Shen Quanqi 80
Shijing xix–xx, 57, 66–67, 70–72, 75, 83, 97
Sikong Tu 33
Sima Xiangru 7, 97
simplicity xvi–xvii, xxiv–vi, 20, 28, 35, 37, 47, 50, 68, 69
Song Jing 4, 5
Song Yu viii, xxiii
Su Dongpo 28, 32, 74
Su Shi 74
Sunny Pass 84, 91, 101

Index   119

sunset 21, 49, 53, 57, 64, 84, 91, 95, 100–102
symbol xix, xxi, xxiii–iv, 46–47, 50–51, 90, 103

Taizong 3, 4, 6, 43, 50
Tang poetry i, v–viii, x, xii–xvi, xix, xxii, xxiv, xxvi–viii, 20, 23–25, 28, 36–37, 39, 40, 42–54, 56, 68–96, 106, 109, 111
Tao Yuanming 29–30, 59, 61–62, 66, 74–75, 79, 83, 98–99, 101–111
Tianbao 22
Turks 4, 50
Turpan 4, 50

Wang Can 73, 75
Wang Changling xv, xxii, 38, 39, 51–53, 82, 84, 92, 98, 100
Wang Ji 21
Wang Wei xiii–xiv, xxviii, 37, 52, 53, 60–62, 65, 81, 84, 87, 91, 93, 98, 100–101
Wang Zhihuan 61, 67, 98, 100
water xiv, 34, 37–38, 48, 49, 51, 53, 56, 61–62, 64–66, 78, 82–83, 86, 92–93, 99, 101–102
Weicheng 84, 91, 101
White Emperor 67
white hair xv, 39–40
white sun 12–13, 15, 22, 26, 61, 100
willow xxii, 45, 76, 83–84, 92, 98–99, 101–102
wind vi, xii, xv, xxii–iii, 7–8, 12, 15–16, 18, 26, 31, 37, 38, 40, 48, 51–53, 55, 57, 60–62, 78, 81, 84, 94–95, 98–100, 102

wine 30, 37, 39, 47, 53, 66, 81, 83–84, 91, 93, 95, 101–102
Wu Zetian 2–7, 18, 21

Xianyang 37, 53, 81
Xie Lingyun 32, 58–60, 62–64, 74
Xie Tiao 24, 57, 59, 64
Xuanzong 3–4
Xue Daoheng 99

Yan Yu xv–xvi, 29, 43
Yangtze River xxvi, 39, 49, 63, 78, 91
Yanshan 111
Yao Chong 4–6
Yelang 49
Yellow Crane Tower 49, 90–91
Yellow River 26, 39, 57, 96, 98, 100
Yin Fan xvi, 25, 27
Youth Spirit i, xi, xiv, xxviii, 81, 109
Youzhou 5, 16–18, 23–24, 39, 95
Yu Xin 45, 73, 76–77, 88, 98
Yuan Haowen 8, 9
Yuanhe 1
Yuanjia 56, 63–64
yuefu 37, 57, 72, 86, 94–95, 101
Yumen 61, 98, 101

Zhang Jianzhi 4
Zhang Jiuling 12
Zhang Ruoxu 47
Zhenguan 3–5, 21, 43, 50
Zhong Rong 7, 24, 29, 34
Zhongnan 65, 67, 87
Zhu Yizun 28
Zu Yong 67
Zuo Si 29, 30, 62, 98

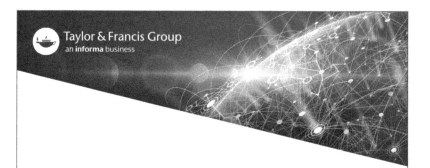